BIBLEMAN®
BIBLE STORYBOOK

by MIKE NAPPA

illustrations by
Dennis Edwards

B&H
KIDS

CONTENTS

THE ARMOR OF GOD

Finally, be strengthened by the Lord and by his vast strength. Put on the full armor of God so that you can stand against the schemes of the devil. For our struggle is not against flesh and blood, but against the rulers, against the authorities, against the cosmic powers of this darkness, against evil, spiritual forces in the heavens. For this reason take up the full armor of God, so that you may be able to resist in the evil day, and having prepared everything, to take your stand. Stand, therefore, with truth like a belt around your waist, righteousness like armor on your chest, and your feet sandaled with readiness for the gospel of peace. In every situation take up the shield of faith with which you can extinguish all the flaming arrows of the evil one. Take the helmet of salvation and the sword of the Spirit—which is the word of God.

—*Ephesians 6:10–17*

Meet the Bibleteam!

Bibleman
Josh Carpenter

MY GOAL: To lead kids to Jesus Christ.

TACTICS: I teach Bible stories that relate to kids' situations, and I defeat villains with Scripture.

FAVE SCRIPTURE: Ephesians 6:10–17

WEAPON OF CHOICE: The sword of the Spirit (the Word of God)

HOBBY: Riding motorcycles

FAVE SLUSH-EZ FLAVOR: Bubblegum-java-mint

Biblegirl
Lia Martin

MY GOAL: To protect kids from the enemies of God!

TACTICS: I develop Bible lessons, and I oppose villains.

FAVE SCRIPTURE: Philippians 4:8–9

WEAPON OF CHOICE: Dual light-tonfas (used with God's Word)

HOBBY: Music and singing

FAVE SLUSH-EZ FLAVOR: Strawberry-chocolate

Cypher
Kerry Turner, "KT"

MY GOAL: To help kids live for Jesus Christ.

TACTICS: I use innovative media and technology to defeat villains.

FAVE SCRIPTURE:
2 Timothy 2:15

WEAPON OF CHOICE:
Light-bo staff (used with God's Word)

HOBBY: Writing computer code and tweaking processors

FAVE SLUSH-EZ FLAVOR:
Cantaloupe-bubblegum

Melody

MY GOAL: To help advance the Bibleteam's mission.

TACTICS: As a rookie, I assist the Bibleteam with vehicle operation and technology monitoring.

FAVE SCRIPTURE:
Colossians 3:23–25

WEAPON OF CHOICE:
Dual light-escrima (used with God's Word)

HOBBY: Gymnastics

FAVE SLUSH-EZ FLAVOR:
Kiwi-lemon swirl

Bibleman!
The Official Theme Song

Bibleman! Bibleman!
Fighting for the way, he's the Bibleman.

Bibleman! Fighting the good fight,
Taking the shield of faith and the belt of truth,
Bibleman is on the move.
The sword of the Spirit is the Word of God.
There's nothing it can't do.

Bibleman! Bibleman!
Fighting the good fight,
Wearing the breastplate of righteousness
  and the helmet of salvation.
Biblegirl, Cypher, and Melody—
Fighting for the way.

We stand together in the sight of God.
We stand together to do what's right.

Bibleman! Bibleman!
Fighting for God's truth and way!

OLD TESTAMENT ADVENTURES

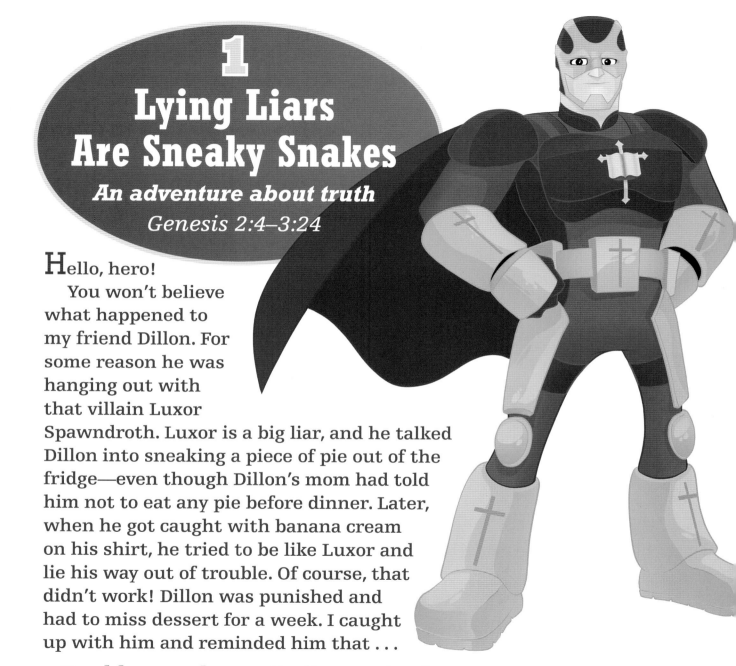

1
Lying Liars Are Sneaky Snakes

An adventure about truth

Genesis 2:4–3:24

Hello, hero! You won't believe what happened to my friend Dillon. For some reason he was hanging out with that villain Luxor Spawndroth. Luxor is a big liar, and he talked Dillon into sneaking a piece of pie out of the fridge—even though Dillon's mom had told him not to eat any pie before dinner. Later, when he got caught with banana cream on his shirt, he tried to be like Luxor and lie his way out of trouble. Of course, that didn't work! Dillon was punished and had to miss dessert for a week. I caught up with him and reminded him that . . .

Real heroes know God's way is always true.

We learned that from Adam and Eve. . . .

It was back at the beginning of the world…

God had created every-thing—animals, trees, plants, and even the first humans.

Adam and Eve lived in God's awesome garden, a place called Eden. It was perfect, full of happiness and peace and everything Adam or Eve could ever want. And they were in charge of it all! Wow!

The only rule God gave them was that Adam and Eve could not eat fruit from one special tree. But God had an enemy in the garden: a sneaky serpent. That nasty villain knew he could never defeat God, but he thought maybe he could ruin things for God's creation instead. So he set his sights on Adam and Eve.

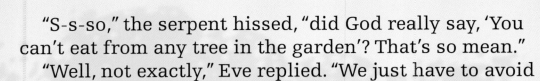

"S-s-so," the serpent hissed, "did God really say, 'You can't eat from any tree in the garden'? That's so mean."

"Well, not exactly," Eve replied. "We just have to avoid this one tree. We can't even touch it."

"God's way is too s-s-s-strict," the serpent said. He was lying—big-time—and he just kept going. "Eating this fruit will make you happy," he said. "You'll be like God! Go ahead, eat it!"

Hmm, Eve thought. *Maybe God's way isn't true after all.* The serpent had fooled her, and she took a bite. Adam did too.

"Uh-oh," said Adam. "I think we've made a big mistake."

"I'm so embarrassed," Eve said.

The serpent just laughed. "I can't believe you fell for my big lies!"

Then God came to the garden for His daily visit. "Adam!" God called out. "Where are you?"

"Ummm," Adam said. "Oops," said Eve. "Yikes!" said the serpent.

At first Adam and Eve tried to hide from God, but that didn't work. God found them, and soon they confessed to everything. They realized the awful thing they'd done. God had been so good to them! But they'd chosen to listen to the serpent's lie instead of sticking to God's true way.

God was so disappointed because He knew what would happen next.

Because of their sin, Adam and Eve could no longer live forever in God's wonderful garden. They had to leave, and one day they would die.

God placed an angel with a flaming, whirling sword outside the garden to be a guard. And no one was ever allowed back into Eden again.

Bibleman says,

Reading about Adam and Eve can teach us a big lesson about believing the truth and telling the truth. After his whole experience with the pie, my friend Dillon decided not to hang out with Luxor anymore. Dillon told me, "Adam and Eve had a hard time believing that God's way is always true. I know I can't be perfect, but I am going to try to remember that God's way is true no matter what. That's what a real hero would do!"

So Dillon told Luxor to stop telling him to do what was wrong and to get lost! At last, that evil villain was defeated.

Bibleteam Challenge

Wouldn't it be great if someone could always remind you to avoid the lies of temptation and live by God's truth instead? Someone can . . . you!

Together with a parent, make a video of you reciting Psalm 86:11.

Try different accents, wear a cool costume, whatever seems fun. Each night this week, right before bed, replay your video as part of your nightly prayers. Amen!

*Teach me your way, Lord,
and I will live by your truth.*
—Psalm 86:11

2
Noah, Build That Boat!
An adventure about faithfulness
Genesis 6:9–9:17

Hey there, hero!

Have you heard of the Shadow of Doubt? He's a villain who spreads doubt and confusion about God's plans for us. Crazy, huh? Well, last week the Shadow of Doubt showed up at church, talking nonsense. "Does God want you to pray every day? And read your Bible?" he asked. "I doubt it! Let's make our birthday lists instead."

Alarm bells went off here at Bibleteam headquarters, so Melody raced to the church to help out. She told everyone about Noah in the Bible and how he reminds us that . . .

Real heroes are faithful to God's plan.

Noah lived in a time when everyone had quit doing what was right—but he remained faithful to God anyway. One day God spoke to Noah. "Make yourself an ark," God said. "I'm bringing a great flood."

Building an ark was a BIG job. That boat was as big as a five-story building! If you took the wings off, you could've parked two airplanes end-to-end inside of it. It was so big that it took Noah and his family years and years and years to finish the work.

Noah probably felt like doubting God's instructions sometimes. Maybe there were times he felt like giving up. But Noah knew real heroes are faithful to God's plan, so he kept working, every day, day after day, slowly building a giant, wooden ark.

And then it was time.

God sent all kinds of animals to join Noah's family in the ark. They came in pairs: birds and bugs, gorillas and giraffes, donkeys and dogs and lions and lambs and tigers and turtles and even a few cats.

Noah was so glad he'd kept working! They were ready. The rain was coming, but they were safe in the ark.

And that's when God shut the door.

Pfassshh! Whoo-oosh! Crish-crasshh!
The ocean floor cracked open, and flooding water burst out all over the planet. A mighty storm covered the earth with rain for forty days and forty nights. The waters rose higher and higher until the land totally disappeared underneath it all.

Finally the rain and flooding water stopped. Only Noah and those with him on the ark survived the flood. Their boat drifted for days and days, then weeks, then months. After 150 days, the floodwaters finally drew back, leaving Noah's ark to rest on Mount Ararat.

When Noah and his family came out of the big boat, they were glad they'd been faithful to God's plan. They found a fresh new world waiting for them—and God's promise, shining in the sky. A rainbow! It was a sign that God would never again destroy the entire world with a flood.

Cypher says,

Noah sure was faithful, even when he was stuck on a boat with all those smelly animals for a looooong time. Whew! I don't even like the smell of one wet dog . . . Anyway, I see why Melody used this story to battle the Shadow of Doubt.

When Melody reminded everyone of Noah's faithfulness during the Great Flood, it broke the curse of the Shadow of Doubt! Kids all over chose to be faithful again about reading the Bible and praying each day—just as God planned for His followers. Yay!

Bibleteam Challenge

Be like Noah: build a boat! Cut off the egg-shaped spaces in the bottom of an egg carton (get a parent to help!) to make the boat's body. Next, poke a long toothpick into the middle of the egg spaces—this will be the mast. Cut a piece of paper for a sail. Write Revelation 2:19 on the sail, and use tape to attach the sail to the toothpick-mast. Now fill up the sink and sail your boat, Noah!

I know your works—
your love, faithfulness,
service, and endurance.
—Revelation 2:19

3

A Babe for Abe

An adventure about patience

Genesis 12–13, 15, 21:1–6

Howdy, hero!

What would you do in this situation? Genevieve had just moved to a new school, far away from all her friends. Her mom told her to be patient and wait for God to bring new friends into her life, but the Whiner Brothers said she should pout and whine and complain about moving instead. I knew it was time to act! I visited Genevieve and reminded her that Abraham showed us . . .

Real heroes are willing to wait for good things.

Here's what happened with Abraham. . . .

A long, long time ago, Abraham lived in a place called Ur. One day God told Abe to take his family and move to a land called Canaan. God promised that in Canaan, Abraham's family would grow and his children would become a great nation!

Well, Abraham thought that sounded pretty cool, so he packed up his wife, Sarah, their servants, their animals—everything!—and off they went. The only problem was that Abraham's wife couldn't have even one child. How was God supposed to keep His promise? Hmm.

Abraham got to his new home in Canaan, and he waited. Nothing happened. Sarah waited. Still nothing. Years passed . . .

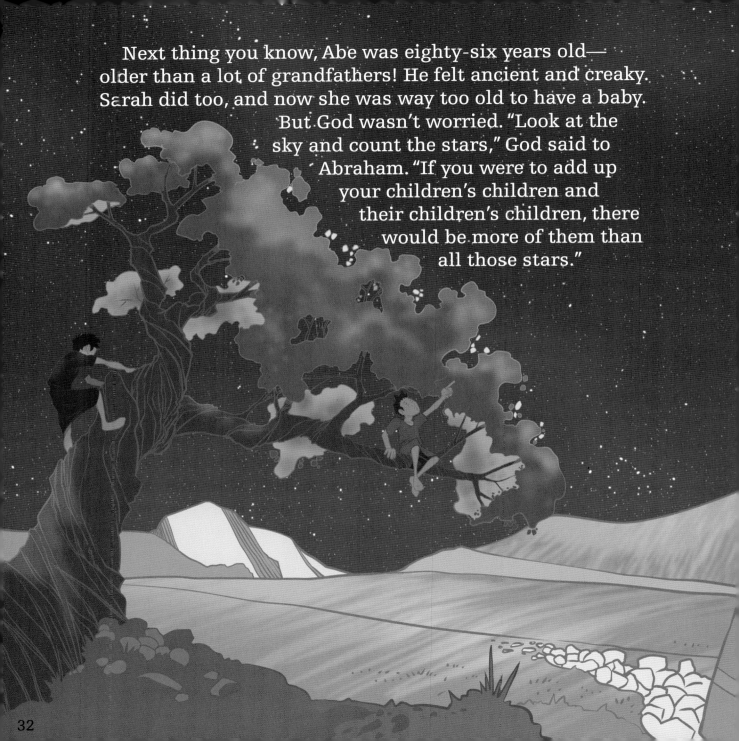

Next thing you know, Abe was eighty-six years old—
older than a lot of grandfathers! He felt ancient and creaky.
Sarah did too, and now she was way too old to have a baby.
But God wasn't worried. "Look at the
sky and count the stars," God said to
Abraham. "If you were to add up
your children's children and
their children's children, there
would be more of them than
all those stars."

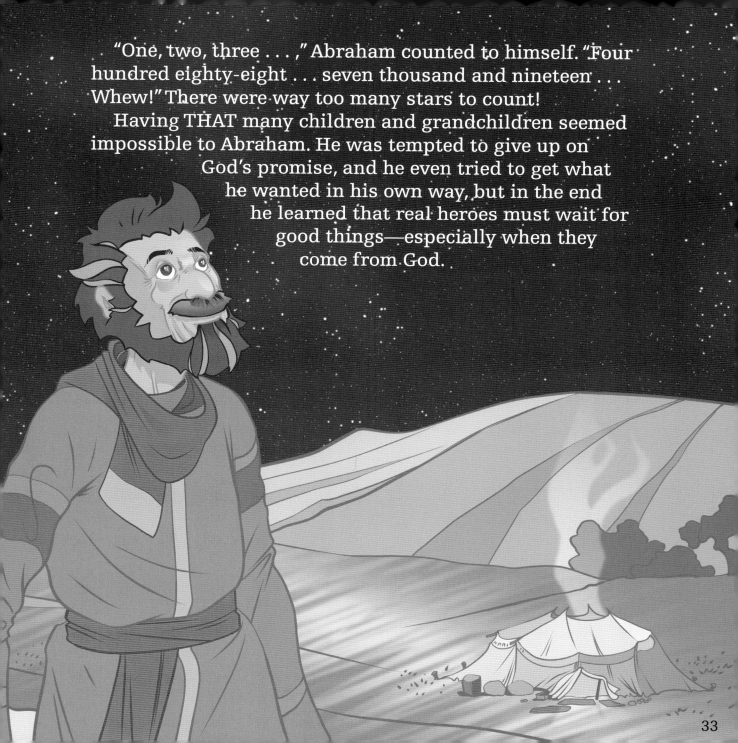

"One, two, three . . . ," Abraham counted to himself. "Four hundred eighty-eight . . . seven thousand and nineteen . . . Whew!" There were way too many stars to count!

Having THAT many children and grandchildren seemed impossible to Abraham. He was tempted to give up on God's promise, and he even tried to get what he wanted in his own way, but in the end he learned that real heroes must wait for good things—especially when they come from God.

Another year passed. Then five more. Then ten. Then fourteen!
But Abraham trusted God and, you guessed it, kept waiting.
When Abraham was one hundred—old enough to be a great-great-grandfather!—a miracle happened.

Sarah and Abe became the proud parents of a beautiful little boy.

"God has brought me laughter!" Sarah said as she held her new baby. And so they named the boy Isaac, which means "laughter." They were both so happy God had brought this wonderful child into their lives.

Isaac became the first of many, many children and grandchildren and great-grandchildren for Abraham—including Jesus. Counting from that time to today, Abraham's children might already number more than the stars in the sky! God's promises are always worth waiting for.

Biblegirl says,

When my friend Genevieve wanted to complain about having to move away from her friends, reading about Abraham helped her learn that real heroes are willing to wait for good things. She ignored the Whiner Brothers and waited patiently for God to bring new friends into her life. And God did!

Bibleteam Challenge

Think you'd be any good at waiting for a promise? Ask a parent to help you set a timer for one minute. Try your best to sit quietly as you wait for the timer to buzz.

How'd you do?

Next set the timer for three minutes. Then for five minutes. Was that easier or harder? Why?

Finish your "waiting test" with a prayer: "Jesus, please help me wait patiently for the Lord. Amen!"

Wait for the Lord; be strong, and let your heart be courageous. Wait for the Lord.
—Psalm 27:14

Bad News Brothers

An adventure about honesty

Genesis 25:19–35; 27:1–45

Hi-ya, hero!

Do you ever get mad at your brother or sister? One time my friend Alexander was losing a game with his sister. He got so angry that the Ronin of Wrong talked him into cheating! Alex had forgotten that . . .

Real heroes don't cheat.

So I told him about Jacob and Esau. . . .

Jacob and Esau were twin brothers, sons of Isaac and Rebekah.

Esau was born first, so it was his birthright to become the leader of their family one day.

That made Jacob angry.

One day Esau was exhausted and weak from hunting.

He needed food—fast!

Jacob saw a chance to steal his brother's birthright. He had some yummy food but refused to share with Esau unless his brother gave up his right to be the head of the family one day. Esau was so hungry that he agreed.

But both brothers knew Esau had been cheated.

The years passed, and their father, Isaac, was now very old and could no longer see anything. One day he decided it was time to share a special blessing with his firstborn son, Esau.

Jacob and his mother found out about what Isaac was going to do, and they devised a secret plan to cheat Esau out of the blessing.

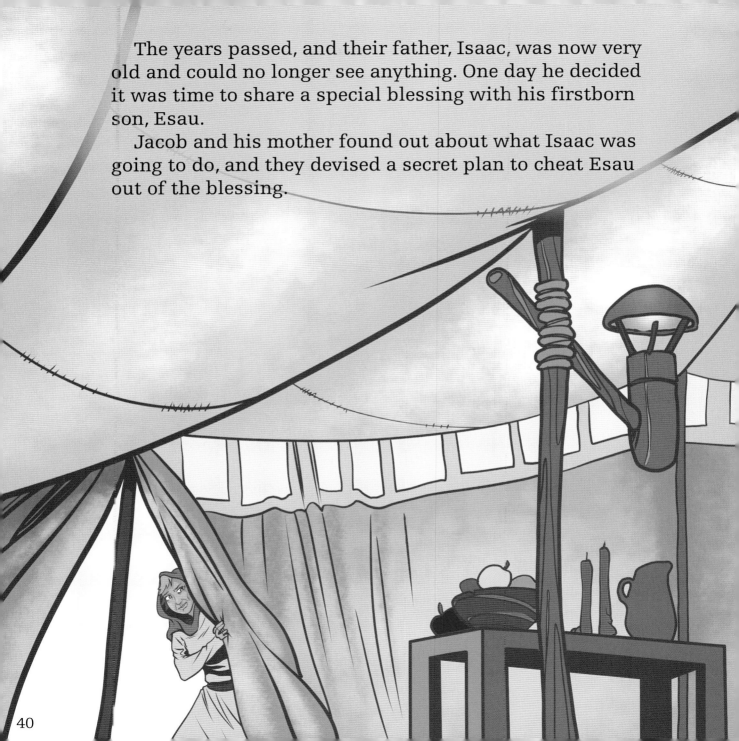

Jacob dressed in Esau's clothes and even put fur on his hands and neck so he'd smell and feel like Esau (who was a hairy guy). Then Jacob took some of his mother's cooking to Isaac and lied to his father, saying, "I am Esau, your firstborn. Give me your blessing."

Blind Isaac was fooled! He gave Esau's blessing to Jacob.

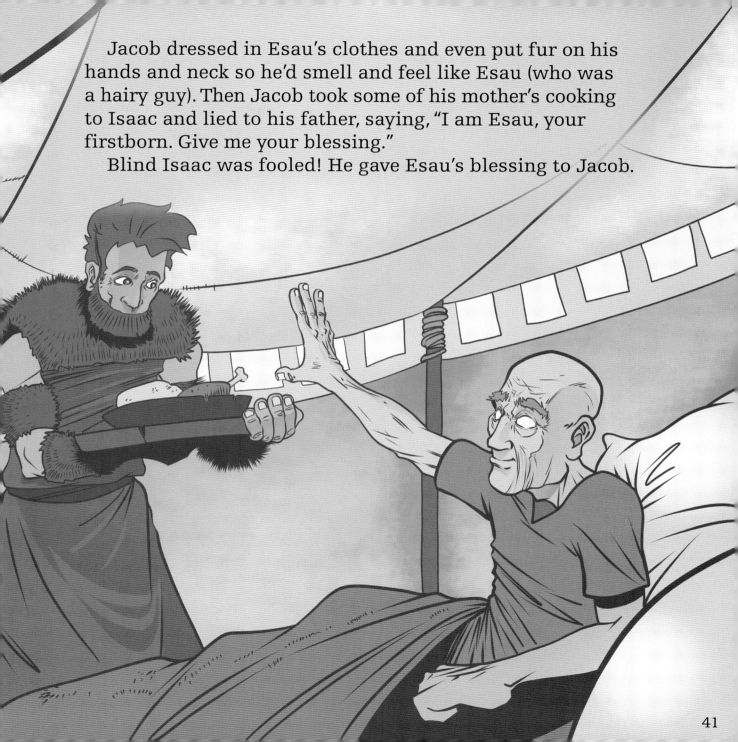

When Esau found out what his brother had done, he was furious!

"Where's Jacob?" he roared. "My brother has cheated me for the last time."

Esau made plans for revenge. *I'm going to kill that little cheater Jacob*, he decided, *and no one will be able to stop me.*

Well, Jacob knew he'd gone too far, but it was too late. Esau was now his enemy. What could he do? Jacob ran, ran, ran away.

After that, Jacob spent most of his life thinking his brother wanted to kill him! It was many years before the two ever saw each other again.

Melody says,

Thankfully, Esau forgave Jacob in the end, but it was a long time before that happened.

The good news is that my friend Alexander learned Jacob's lesson: real heroes don't cheat. He apologized to his sister, played the game fair and square, and decided never to listen to the Ronin of Wrong again.

Bibleteam Challenge

Think about your favorite game. Got it? Now, can you name three rules of that game? What happens when players refuse to play by those rules? Is the game more fun or less fun? Why?

The next time you're tempted to cheat someone, remember your favorite game and how God wants you to always treat others the way you would like to be treated.

Just as you want others to do for you, do the same for them.
—*Luke 6:31*

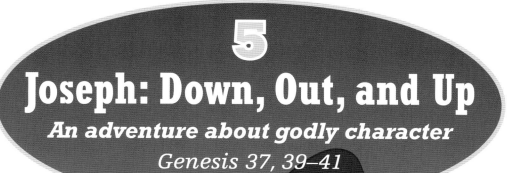

5

Joseph: Down, Out, and Up

An adventure about godly character

Genesis 37, 39–41

Hello, hero!
What would you do if you were punished, but you'd done nothing wrong? Believe it or not, that's exactly what happened to Joseph in the Bible! Let's look at his story as we learn this truth:

Real heroes live for God in both good times and bad.

Joseph was one of Jacob's sons. He had one younger brother and ten older brothers, but Joseph was his father's favorite. That made his older brothers angry, and they were often mean to him.

One day God gave Joseph a dream about bundles of grain. In it, his family's grain bowed down to his grain, like he was a king! It was awesome.

Joseph was so excited that he told his brothers about the dream. He thought they'd be happy for him.

They were not happy.

In fact, they were so mad about it, one day they tied up Joseph and threw him into a pit. And when a band of traveling strangers came by, Joseph's brothers sold him as a slave! Then they lied to their father and said Joseph had been killed by a wild animal.

Meanwhile, those strangers took poor Joseph far, far away to Egypt.

Joseph was scared and sad. He'd done nothing wrong, but he was a slave in Egypt anyway! Still, he knew that real heroes live for God in both good times and bad. Joseph kept praying, kept trying to do what was right, and kept relying on God to help and guide him. And he tried to be a really good servant. That worked great—until his master's wife lied and had Joseph thrown in jail.

It was awful in prison. The cell was cold and lonely, and the guards were sometimes mean.

But even there, Joseph still loved God and tried to live in a way that honored God and helped others.

One day two other prisoners, a baker and a drink-server, told Joseph about dreams they'd had. With God's help, Joseph explained what their dreams meant. Three days later, the drink-server was freed! He went back to work for Pharaoh, the king of Egypt.

Joseph, though, was stuck in prison. He missed his father. He missed eating food that wasn't stinky. He missed being warm in his bed. He probably even missed taking baths!

But Joseph kept praying and relying on God anyway. He knew God still cared about him—and Joseph still cared about God. And guess what? God helped Joseph, even in that dirty prison. Pretty soon the prison warden was his friend too.

Then one day Pharaoh had a strange dream about fat cows and skinny cows but didn't know what it meant. Pharaoh's drink-server remembered Joseph and brought him to see the king.

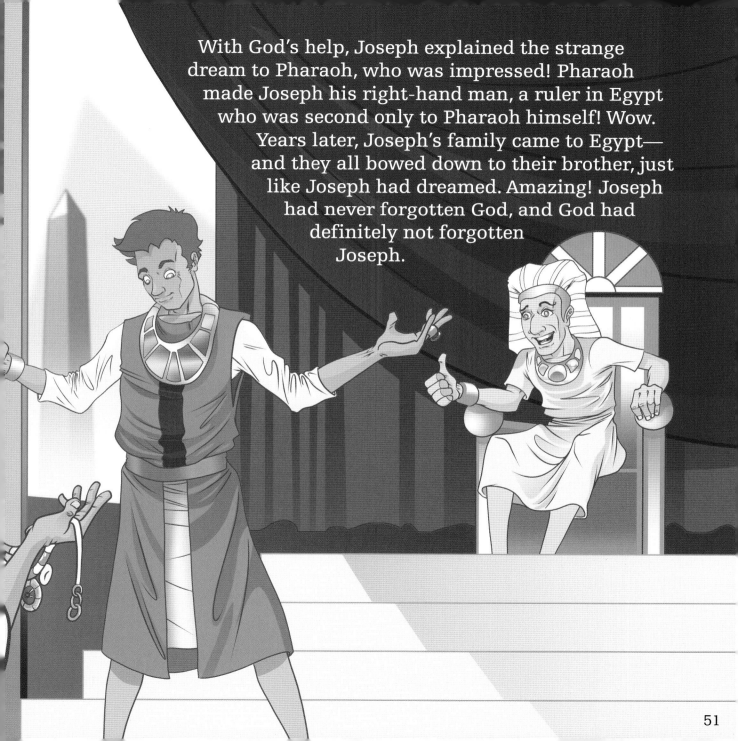

With God's help, Joseph explained the strange dream to Pharaoh, who was impressed! Pharaoh made Joseph his right-hand man, a ruler in Egypt who was second only to Pharaoh himself! Wow. Years later, Joseph's family came to Egypt— and they all bowed down to their brother, just like Joseph had dreamed. Amazing! Joseph had never forgotten God, and God had definitely not forgotten Joseph.

Bibleman says,

Joseph was a real hero.

Are you curious about what he did after he became a rich and powerful ruler? Well, he kept living for God in both good times and bad. He kept praying, trying to do what was right, and relying on God to help and guide him. And guess what? You can do the same.

Bibleteam Challenge

What if Joseph was a superhero? What kind of costume would he wear?

Take some markers and paper and design a superhero logo for Joseph. Then ask a parent to help you use fabric paint to draw your logo onto a white T-shirt. Add Colossians 3:17 to your tee, and then wear it under an overshirt for fun. Whenever you tear open your overshirt to reveal your superhero T-shirt, shout out the scripture and tell people you learned it from the heroic story of Joseph!

Whatever you do, in word or in deed, do everything in the name of the Lord Jesus.
—*Colossians 3:17*

6
Moses: Let My People Go
An adventure about God's will
Exodus 3–15

Hi-ya, hero!

Were you around when the Grand Duchess of Greed started making jewelry? It was crazy. She got a whole bunch of kids to wear bracelets that said, "WIIFM?" She wanted kids to ask themselves, "What's In It For Me?" before they did anything. Just crazy!

Those of us on the Bibleteam knew we had to do something because . . .

Real heroes ask, "What does God want me to do?"

So we reminded everyone of what happened with Moses in the Bible. . . .

Moses lived in Egypt, where Pharaoh was the mean ruler of all the land. In that time all the Hebrews were slaves to Pharaoh—and Moses was a Hebrew! That was *not* good.

When Moses was a baby, though, God worked it out so that he was adopted by Pharaoh's daughter. He lived like a prince with the royal family. Even so, when he grew to be a man, he left Egypt and moved away to a place called Midian. He lived happily as a shepherd there. Problem was, the rest of the Hebrews were still stuck in Egypt—as slaves!

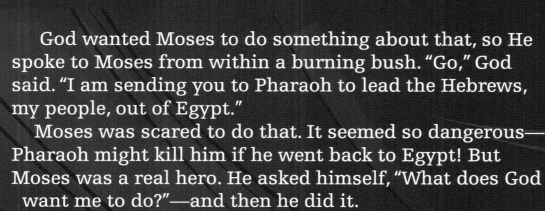

God wanted Moses to do something about that, so He spoke to Moses from within a burning bush. "Go," God said. "I am sending you to Pharaoh to lead the Hebrews, my people, out of Egypt."

Moses was scared to do that. It seemed so dangerous—Pharaoh might kill him if he went back to Egypt! But Moses was a real hero. He asked himself, "What does God want me to do?"—and then he did it.

So Moses headed back to Egypt. He met up with his brother, Aaron, and the two of them went to Pharaoh and said, "This is what the Lord says: 'Let My people go!'"

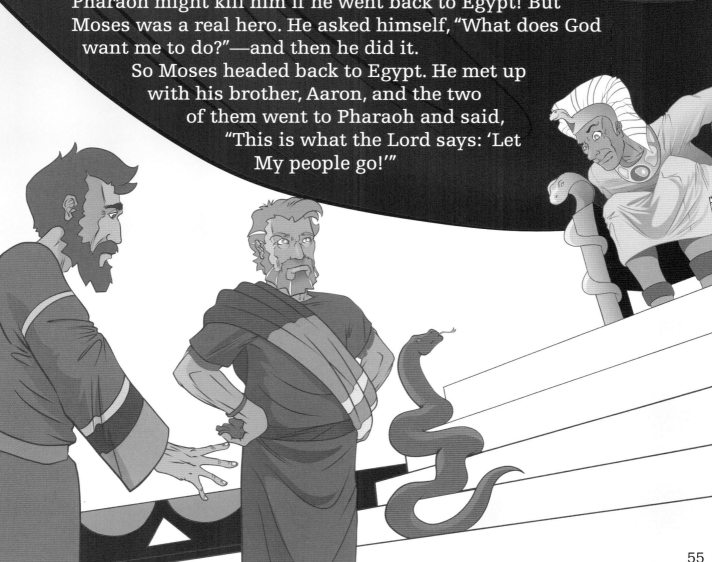

"Why should I do anything for the Lord?" Pharaoh said. "What's in it for me? You're all just slackers! Get back to work!" Then he punished the slaves and made them work harder.

God didn't like that. Not at all.

To convince Pharaoh to set His people free, God sent ten plagues, each one worse than the last. They were:

1. Blood in the Egyptians' drinking water. (Gross!)
2. Millions of frogs, getting into everything—even Pharaoh's underwear drawer.
3. A zillion tiny little gnats, bug-bug-bugging the Egyptians, swarming into their ears and noses, and giving people bad gnat-breath.
4. Gadzillions of flies, buzzing around the Egyptians' faces day and night.

5. Sick cows and donkeys and camels, dying everywhere and stinking up all of Egypt.
6. Painful skin sores.
7. A crashing, smashing hail storm.
8. A locust attack that ate up all the plants and food.
9. Three full days of darkness—nighttime all the time!
10. And finally, worst of all, God sent the angel of death into Egypt. It was awful.

After the last plague, Pharaoh had finally had enough. He was exhausted from trying to fight with God.

"Get out," he said to Moses and Aaron, "you and the Hebrews. Go worship the Lord."

Pharaoh set God's people free! Sort of.

The Hebrews all headed away from Egypt, but when Pharaoh saw them leaving, he changed his mind. He called together his soldiers, and they chased after God's people.

Moses and his people were trapped! In front of them was the Red Sea, and behind them was the Egyptian army. "No problem," God said. He pushed aside all the water so that Moses and the people could walk through on dry land. Wow!

But when Pharaoh and his army tried to follow . . . well, God made the water crash back down right on top of them. The Hebrews were finally free from Pharaoh!

Melody says,

When we remember that Moses did what God wanted, it reminds us to also make good choices. Pharaoh only thought about himself, but Moses thought about God first. By following God's will, Moses freed his people from slavery. Talk about a real hero!

After we reminded everyone of what happened with Moses in the Bible, the Grand Duchess of Greed went out of business overnight! Kids started asking, "What does God want me to do?"—and then they chucked those silly "WIIFM?" bracelets into the trash where they belonged.

Bibleteam Challenge

Make "Green Means Follow God!" cuff bracelets for your family. First, get a parent or older sibling to help. Next, cut a cardboard paper-towel tube into four equal pieces—these will be your "cuffs." (Use an extra tube if you have more than four people in your family.)

To make a bracelet, (1) Cut one of the tube pieces top to bottom, lengthwise, to form a cuff. (2) Tape one end of a roll of green yarn to the cuff, then wrap the yarn around the cuff in a crisscross pattern until it's covered in green. (3) Tie off or tape the end of the yarn to finish your bracelet! Wear these "Green Means Follow God!" bracelets to remind everyone in your home to make good choices every day.

The one who does the will of God remains forever.
—1 John 2:17

7
Joshua's Long Walk

*An adventure about
facing obstacles*
Joshua 6

Hi there, hero!

Ever feel like something is just too hard, that you can't ever win? I have.

When I was younger I was diagnosed with ADHD—Attention Deficit Hyperactivity Disorder. That meant I had trouble paying attention and sitting still, and school was really hard for me. The Shadow of Doubt crept up and told me ADHD was like a giant wall that I'd never get over!

Then Bibleman came to see me. He told me about Joshua and how . . .

Real heroes know that God can do anything.

After Moses died, God chose Joshua to take charge of His people. Joshua led the Israelites (the Hebrews) into Canaan, the land that God had promised them.

They ran into a big obstacle right away—the city of Jericho. The people there didn't want the Israelites in Canaan, so Joshua had to figure out a way to defeat that city. But Jericho was surrounded by a huge wall that nobody could knock down.

What was he going to do?

As Joshua was wondering how to defeat Jericho, an angel of the Lord appeared. He promised that God would take care of that big, strong wall and give the Israelites victory over Jericho. Then the angel gave Joshua some really unusual instructions from God:

"March around the city once a day, for six straight days," the angel said. "On the seventh day, march around Jericho seven times. Then have the priests blow their trumpets loudly, and tell all your soldiers to shout!"

Joshua looked at the wall of Jericho. It was so big. God wanted His army to walk around, blow trumpets, and shout? How was that supposed to defeat the city of Jericho? Hmm.

Then Joshua remembered that God can do ANYTHING. No obstacle was ever going to be too hard for God to overcome. So Joshua did just what the angel instructed . . .

And the walls of Jericho came crumbling down!

Cypher says,

Hearing about what God did for Joshua really made a difference in my attitude! I realized that the Shadow of Doubt was wrong when he tried to tell me I couldn't succeed. Real heroes know that God can do anything!

With God's help, I learned how to study in ways that worked best for me. I learned a lot! And I did better in school. And now I'm part of the Bibleteam! How awesome is that? God really can do *anything!*

Bibleteam Challenge

Draw a picture of Cypher, and have one of your parents write today's Bible Spotlight Verse at the bottom of your drawing. Tape it near your front door.

Every time you and your family leave or enter your house this week, give Cypher a high five and recite aloud Matthew 19:26.

With God all things are possible.
—Matthew 19:26

8
Deborah: Wise Woman of Wonder

An adventure about wisdom

Judges 4–5

Howdy, hero!
Have you ever had to stand up to a bully? It's scary, isn't it? But when the Master of Mean sent a bully to pick on my friend Gabriella's little brother, she knew she had to do something. She just didn't know exactly what to do!

Then she read about Deborah in the Bible and discovered that . . .

Real heroes ask God for wisdom about what to do.

Deborah lived in the land of Canaan, way back before Israel even had a king. She was a wise woman and a judge. She helped the people of Israel settle arguments so they could all live together in peace.

But evil king Jabin and the commander of his army, named Sisera, also lived in Canaan. They were big bullies! They picked on the Israelites every chance they got. They attacked Deborah's people and stole from them, and the Israelites didn't know what to do.

This bullying went on for twenty long years! Deborah kept asking God for wisdom about how to stand up to Jabin and Sisera. One day God showed her a spectacular plan for beating those bullies! She met with Israel's greatest warrior, Barak, and explained it to him.

"Take ten thousand men and go to Mount Tabor," she said. "Sisera's army will come out to fight you. The Lord will lure them into the river and—*Bam!* They'll get stuck, and you will easily defeat them."

Barak didn't like the plan. "I'll only go if you go with me," he said.

"Fine," Deborah said. "But since you don't trust God's wisdom, the greatest honor from this battle will go to a woman instead of you."

They all went to Mount Tabor. Barak still wasn't sure it would work, but Deborah knew that real heroes ask God for wisdom about what to do. She made sure the Israelite army followed God's plan, and . . . *Bam!*

The battle went just as God had said it would! It was a total victory!

Except Sisera got away. But
God had a plan for that too.

Sisera ran like a scared rabbit away from the battle until he came to the tent where a woman named Jael lived. She recognized the evil commander and knew she couldn't let him get away. If he did, then Sisera and Jabin would just build a new army and come back to bully the Israelites all over again.

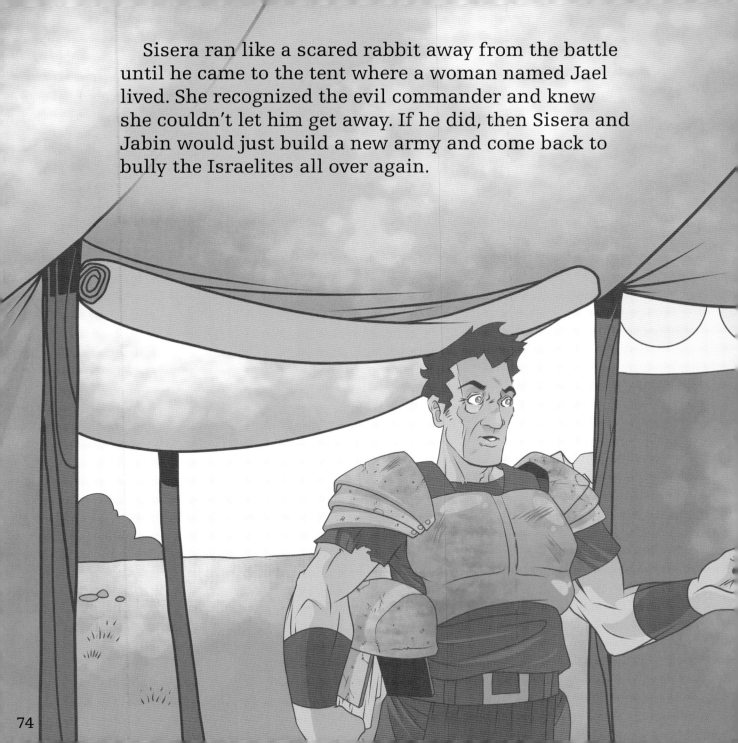

"Come hide in my tent," Jael said to Sisera. Then she waited.

The evil commander was so exhausted that he fell right to sleep, making it easy for Jael to defeat him.

When Barak arrived, still chasing his enemy, Jael greeted him and told him she had already defeated Sisera! God had helped them win!

And just like Deborah had promised, the greatest honor from the battle went to Jael, a woman, instead of to Barak, the army commander.

Gideon lived a long time ago in Israel, near the land of Midian. It was a rough time to be an Israelite because people from Midian were big jerks. They'd send large groups of soldiers into Israel and ruin everything, just because they were selfish and mean.

The Midianites stole stuff. And burned stuff. And broke stuff.

They took any food they could find and stole farm animals like cows and donkeys. There were so many Midianites that the people of Israel were helpless to stop them. It was really annoying.

Like everyone else, Gideon was afraid of the Midianites. He just tried to stay out of their way. One day he was trying to hide some wheat from the Midianites when . . .

Somebody snuck up on him!

It was an angel, delivering a message from God: "Go, Gideon. I want you to deliver Israel from the people of Midian. I'm sending you, and I'll be with you."

Gideon really hoped it was true, but he was still afraid. He put a large sheepskin in the grass at night and prayed, "God, if You truly want me to deliver Israel, then when I wake up in the morning make this sheepskin wet, but make the ground all around it completely dry."

And God did just that.

The next night Gideon prayed, "Lord, if You really want me to deliver Israel, then tomorrow morning make the sheepskin dry and the ground wet."

And God did that too.

After finding the sheepskin just as he'd prayed for it to be, hope grew inside Gideon! He realized that real heroes conquer fear with hope in God, and he called for all the fighting men in Israel to join him. Thousands and thousands came—but God surprised Gideon again.

"That's too many men," God said. "Send a bunch of them home."

So Gideon did.

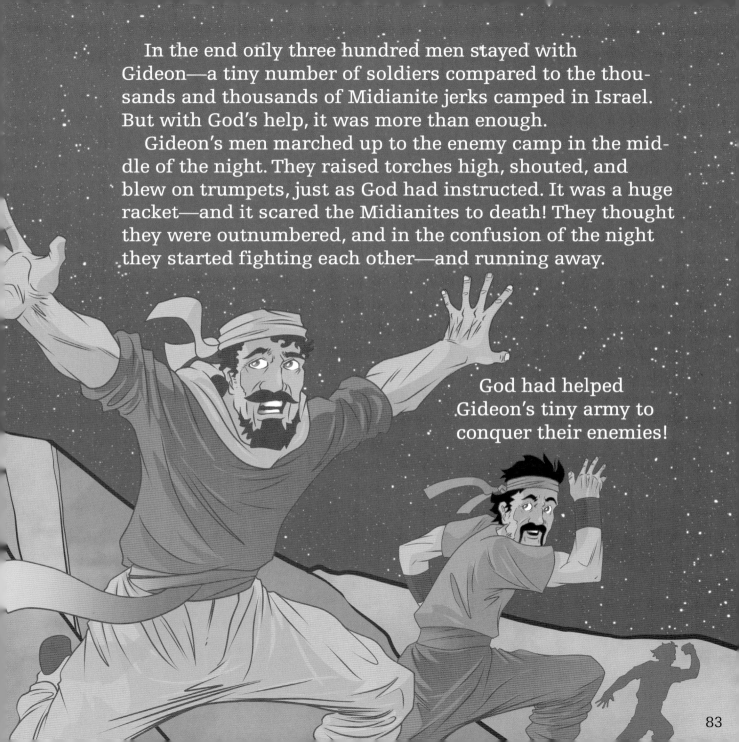

In the end only three hundred men stayed with Gideon—a tiny number of soldiers compared to the thousands and thousands of Midianite jerks camped in Israel. But with God's help, it was more than enough.

Gideon's men marched up to the enemy camp in the middle of the night. They raised torches high, shouted, and blew on trumpets, just as God had instructed. It was a huge racket—and it scared the Midianites to death! They thought they were outnumbered, and in the confusion of the night they started fighting each other—and running away.

God had helped Gideon's tiny army to conquer their enemies!

Bibleman says,

My friend Rose was really glad to hear about Gideon. After all, Gideon was afraid to fight the Midianites—but he was able to conquer his fear with hope from God.

After Rose learned about Gideon, she prayed that God would help her overcome fear while she was at church camp. That prayer of hope scared Dr. Fear! He quit bothering Rose and started looking for someone else to bother instead.

And by the way, that week at camp turned out to be the best seven days of Rose's life! Yay, God!

Bibleteam Challenge

Make this "sheepskin" craft to remind you of Gideon and how real heroes conquer fear with hope in God.

Use a black marker to write "Jeremiah 29:11" on a paper plate. Next, glue cotton balls all over the plate until it looks like a fluffy, funny version of Gideon's sheepskin. At breakfast every day this week, hold up your "sheepskin" and recite Jeremiah 29:11 together with your family. Like Gideon, God has great plans for you!

I know the plans I have for you . . . to give you a future and a hope.
—Jeremiah 29:11

10
The Bigger They Are, The Harder They Fall

An adventure about confidence

1 Samuel 17

Howdy, Hero!

How would you feel if you had to fight a big ol' villain like the Crusher? If you're like the ancient Israelites, you probably would be shaking in your sandals, hiding behind a rock, thinking you were way too small to ever be able to stand up to somebody *that* big.

But if you're like David in the Bible, you know . . .

Real heroes find their confidence in God.

Here's what the Bible tells us about David. . . .

Saul was king in Israel when the Philistine army came to town. There were thousands of them—and they wanted to take over the kingdom.

Saul couldn't allow that, so he gathered the Israelite army and met the Philistines for battle. But there was one big problem. The Philistines had a champion named Goliath who was, well . . .

HUGE! ENORMOUS! A GIANT!

If Goliath were alive today, he'd probably play basketball because he could've dunked a ball without ever having to jump. But he lived back then, so he was a fierce warrior instead. Goliath hated the Israelites, and he didn't care about God either. Every day, for forty days, he came out and roared, "Send me a man so we can fight each other!"

The Israelites looked up, up, up at Goliath, and their confidence went down, down, down. No one thought he could beat Goliath. Nobody was willing to try . . .

. . . Except David.

Now, David wasn't even supposed to be on the battle-field—he was too young. But one day he brought some food to his older brothers and heard Goliath ranting across the field. David was annoyed that no Israelite would stand up to Goliath. He knew that real heroes find their confidence in God! He figured that with God's help, that giant would come a-rumbling and a-tumbling down.

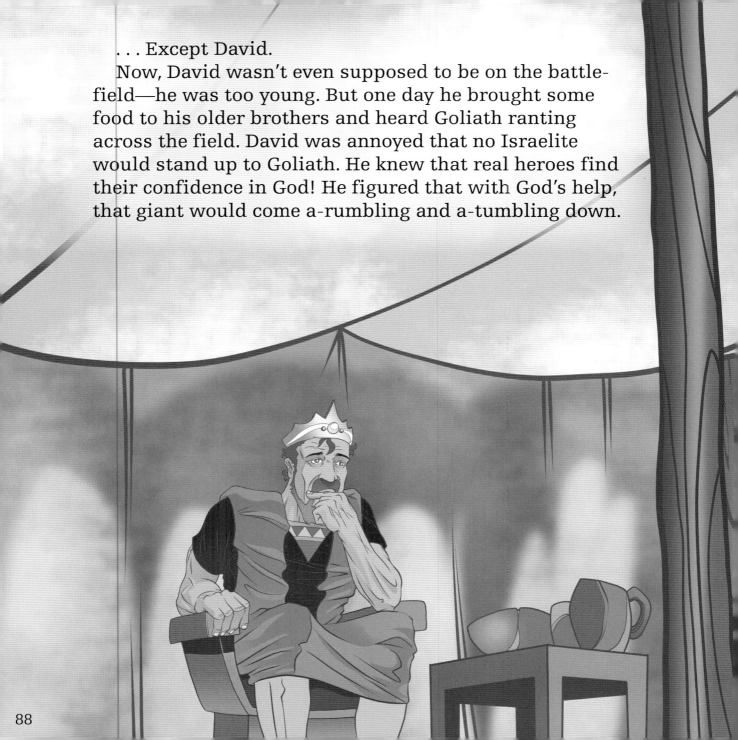

"Who's this guy?" David said. "Does he think he can beat the army of our living God? Pshaw. I'll fight him."

King Saul was glad to hear that somebody—anybody!—was willing to stand up to Goliath. He offered to loan David his own armor for the fight. It didn't fit right, so David made a different plan.

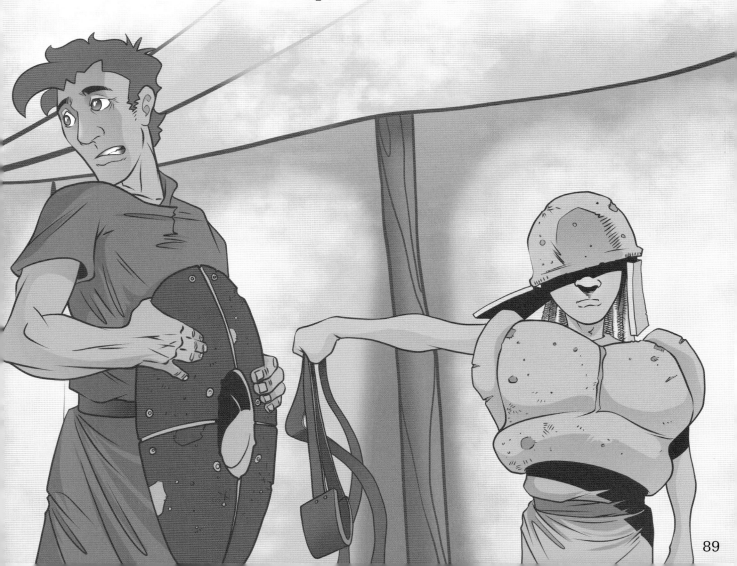

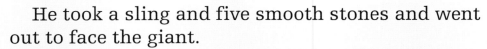

He took a sling and five smooth stones and went out to face the giant.

David didn't waste time on the battlefield. He charged right at Goliath!

"You come against me with a sword, spear, and javelin," David shouted, "but I come against you in the name of God! Today, the Lord will hand you over to me, for the battle is the Lord's!"

David fired a stone from his sling and . . . *Whap!* It hit the giant right in the middle of the forehead.

Goliath rumbled. He stumbled. He tumbled. And down, down, down fell the giant.

With confidence and power from God, David and the whole army of Israel had won!

Biblegirl says,

Wow! That was impressive! Reading about David and Goliath always helps me when I feel unsure about facing something hard in life. David showed everyone in Israel that real heroes find their confidence in God—and he reminds us of that too.

That means that the next time you have to face the Crusher, or you're worried about making a new friend, or you have to do something that makes you feel nervous, you don't have to give up! Like David, you can ask God for help—and find confidence in knowing that God is on your side.

Bibleteam Challenge

Brainstorm with your parents the answer to this question: "Three things I'd like to do but am nervous to try are . . ."

Have your mom or dad write your ideas on separate slips of paper and place them in a bowl. Pray for God to give you confidence, then pick an idea at random from the bowl. Make plans to try it this week!

The battle is the LORD's!
—1 Samuel 17:47

11
A Contest at Carmel
An adventure about loyalty
1 Kings 18:16–40

Hi-ya, hero!

Last summer the Ronin of Wrong came to town. He wanted to convince people it was okay to turn against the Bible's good advice! He promised free video games to every kid who would quit reading the Bible.

Bibleman rushed over to help, but it looked like he was going to be too late. Guess what happened next? A kid just like you stood up! Her name was Anika, and she told everyone:

Real heroes are always on God's side.

Then she read the story of Elijah in the Bible. . . .

Elijah was a prophet of God. He lived in Israel during a time when the evil king Ahab was in charge.

Ahab and his wife, Jezebel, worked hard to lead people away from God. They told everyone to worship a fake god named Baal. Ahab even hired 450 men to be prophets for that fake god. That was like hiring 450 people to be Ronins of Wrong!

Well, after talking to God about it, Elijah went to confront Ahab and those fake prophets.

"Meet me at Mount Carmel," Elijah said to Ahab, "and bring those so-called prophets of Baal too."

They all met on the mountain. A crowd came to watch. There were hundreds of people on Ahab's side, but Elijah was the only prophet on God's side. Elijah knew that was enough.

"Let's have a contest," he said. "You pray to Baal, and then I'll pray to the Lord. The God who answers with fire—He is God!"

The contest was ON!

The prophets of Baal went first. They set up an altar and put meat on it. All morning they prayed to Baal and danced and shouted. Nothing happened.

Elijah yawned. He was getting bored.

"Shout louder," he joked. "Maybe your god is sleeping."

So the prophets of Baal shouted louder. The sun just moved across the sky. They wailed and cried while the day turned toward evening. They screamed and raved and danced and shouted until it was nighttime and they were exhausted.

Nothing happened. No one answered.

"My turn," Elijah said at last.

He took twelve stones and built an altar to the Lord. He put meat on the altar. Then he drenched everything with twelve full pots of water. The altar was soaked! Water dribbled everywhere! Finally, Elijah was ready.

"Lᴏʀᴅ God," he said, "today let it be known that You are God . . ."

Whooossshh!
God sent fire from heaven!
It burned up the meat, the altar, the stones, and even the water. When the people saw it, they fell facedown and said, "The LORD, He is God! The LORD, He is God!"

Melody says,

Remember my friend Anika? After she told her friends about Elijah, the Ronin of Wrong didn't have a chance. "Real heroes are always on God's side," all the kids told him. "Just like Elijah."

By the time Bibleman got there, kids were reading their Bibles again, and the Ronin had already left town. He was no match for real heroes with God's Word!

Bibleteam Challenge

Together with a parent, make a batch of "Elijah Cookies." These are sugar cookies decorated with a "lightning bolt" made of icing. As you're decorating the cookies, talk about these questions: "When does it feel like people try to lead me away from God? What can I do to stay on God's side when that happens?"

When everything's ready, use Romans 8:31 as a cheer—then enjoy your Elijah Cookies!

If God is for us,
who is against us?
—Romans 8:31

12
Bow . . . or Burn?
An adventure about doing what's right
Daniel 3

Hey there, hero!

Did you know the Ambassador of Ignorance once started a rock band? It was called the Rotten Lettuce Band, and his fans called themselves "Lettuceheads." One Sunday morning the band scheduled a big concert and told kids to come to the show instead of church. The Ambassador was trying to lead Lettuceheads into doing what was wrong!

The Bibleteam knew we had to act—fast. So Biblegirl got on the radio and reminded us all that . . .

Real heroes don't let bullies keep them from doing what's right.

Then she broadcast the story of Shadrach, Meshach, and Abednego.

Shadrach, Meshach, and Abednego were servants of Nebuchadnezzar, king of Babylon. Because he was king, Nebuchadnezzar thought everyone should do any foolish thing he dreamed up—no matter what.

First, he ordered his builders to make a *huge* statue of pure gold. Then he made a law that everyone had to bow down and worship his silly statue.

On the grand day, everyone gathered around the statue. The band played, and all the king's servants bowed down . . . except Shadrach, Meshach, and Abednego!

"King Nebuchadnezzar," they said, "it's not right to worship a gold statue. We worship the Lord God only. So even though you're the king, we'll never let you keep us from doing what's right."

The king was furious! "If you won't bow to my statue," he roared, "then you'll burn to death in the fiery furnace. Guards! Take them!"

Things were pretty grim for Shadrach, Meshach, and Abednego. But they knew it was better to die for doing what's right than to live and do what's wrong.

They closed their eyes. They held their breath.

And the guards threw them into the blazing hot furnace.

Then a fantastic thing happened. Something almost unbelievable—but true.

Nebuchadnezzar stared into the furnace, and he blinked. He rubbed his eyes and blinked again. Finally he said, "Um, hey, everybody, didn't we throw three guys into the fire?"

"Yep," the others said.

"Hmm," the king said. "So why do I see four guys walking around in the furnace? And why does that fourth guy look like an angel or something? Uh-oh."

"Shadrach, Meshach, and Abednego!" the king called out. "Servants of the Most High God, come out of there!"

The three guys came out of the furnace—and they were unharmed! Not even a tiny little hair had been burned. None of them even smelled like smoke. It was a massive miracle of God!

"You risked your life to do what was right," Nebuchadnezzar said to them. "You refused to obey a king's command that was wrong, and God saved you! So I hereby decree that from now on, no one will ever say anything bad about the God of Shadrach, Meshach, and Abednego!"

107

Cypher says,

Remembering what happened to Shadrach, Meshach, and Abednego is really encouraging for us today. Sometimes it's hard to follow God, especially when others try to lead us into doing things that are wrong. But hearing about Shadrach, Meshach, and Abednego reminds us that we can be real heroes who don't let anyone keep us from doing what's right.

As for the Ambassador of Ignorance, well, nobody wanted to be his fan after Biblegirl reminded them of the truth. His Sunday-morning concert was a big flop. He stormed out of town and then broke his guitar when he slipped on a pile of rotten lettuce!

Bibleteam Challenge

Have you ever thought to thank the people who help you do what's right? This Sunday, go to church and say, "Thank you!" to three people who encourage you to follow God.

For instance, you could thank your Bible class teacher, your pastor, and the worship leader at your church. For extra fun, draw pictures of Shadrach, Meshach, and Abednego, and include those with your thank-yous!

Put on the full armor of God, so that you can stand against the schemes of the devil.
—*Ephesians 6:11*

13
Something Smells Fishy

An adventure about sharing faith

Jonah 1–3

Hello, hero!

Mr. Malevolent has a strange way of thinking. He hates that God will forgive people who've done something wrong! So recently he tried to prevent Christians from telling others about God's message of love. He started a "No-Share Know-It-Alls" club and tried to get kids to hide their Bibles in his clubhouse. Strange!

The truth is that . . .

Real heroes share God's message with others.

Jonah learned about this the hard way.

Jonah was one of God's prophets a long time ago. He shared God's special messages with people all around him.

One day God told Jonah to go preach in the city of Nineveh. Jonah wasn't happy about that. People in Nineveh were rude and nasty and just plain mean. *If they repent,* he thought, *God will forgive them*. And Jonah didn't really want God to forgive them.

So instead of going to share God's message in Nineveh, he sneaked away on a boat heading in the opposite direction.

But God saw what Jonah was doing. And He still
wanted His prophet to go share the message in Nineveh!
So God sent a storm to rock the boat.

When the sailors found out that Jonah was running from God, they quickly understood what was going on. And they were afraid!

"Throw me overboard," Jonah told them at last. "I deserve it, and then God will calm the storm."

The sailors didn't want to do it, but in the end they threw Jonah into the sea. *Splash!*

And God sent a big fish to catch him.
That fish swallowed Jonah whole and then
began swimming back toward Nineveh, just as
God had originally commanded.

Jonah was miserable inside the belly of that fish. The smell was awful! It was dark! It was slimy! It was cramped! And seaweed got all over Jonah's face!

He prayed to God for help.

After Jonah had been in the fish's belly for three days, God answered his prayer.

The fish spat up Jonah onto dry land. God told Jonah again to go to Nineveh, and you know what? Jonah ran right to Nineveh! On the first day there, he shared God's message with the people, telling them to turn away from doing evil. They immediately did just that! Next, the king of Nineveh joined everyone in praying to God to ask for forgiveness.

God saw that the king and the people had turned away from doing evil. And God forgave them all.

Jonah might have smelled like the stinky inside of a fish's belly, but God had made His point: *real heroes share God's message with others.*

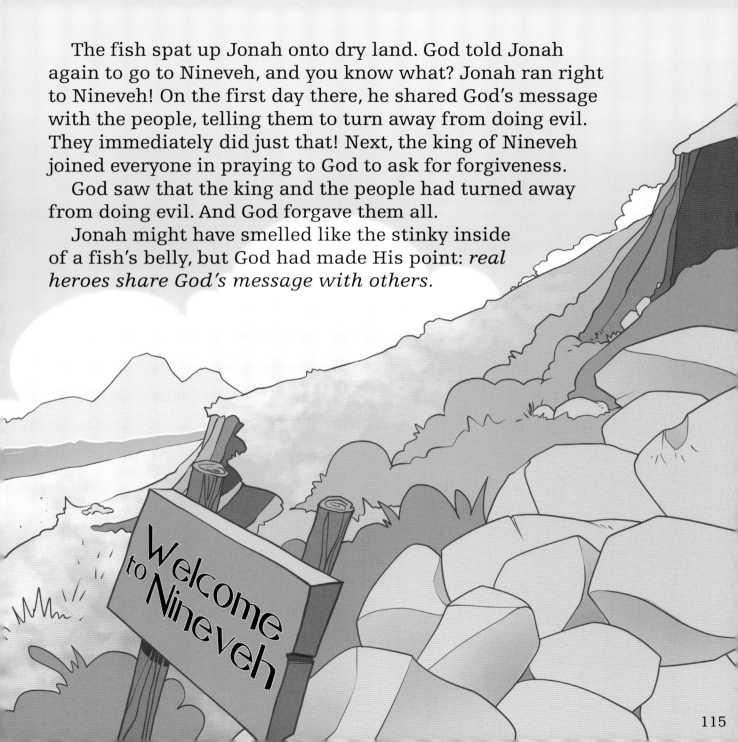

Bibleman says,

Jonah's experience is a great reminder that we shouldn't be "No-Share Know-It-Alls." We don't have to be shy about sharing messages from God's Word. When we tell our friends and family what we're discovering in the Bible, God uses us to help them learn to love and follow Him too!

When kids in town heard about Jonah, they shut down Mr. Malevolent's hateful "No-Share" club. Last I heard, they were sharing the good news from the Bible with him instead!

Bibleteam Challenge

What are three unexpected ways you could share what you learned from Jonah? For instance, you could perform a "Living Room Theatre" show for your family, write a new "Jonah Sea Shanty" to sing to your neighbors, or make a "Jonah Refrigerator Poster" to start conversation when friends come to your house.

Brainstorm ideas, then choose one to share the Bible's message of Jonah with others this week!

Preach the word; be ready in season and out of season.
—2 Timothy 4:2

Did You Know?

- The Bible is an amazing, one-of-a-kind book!

- It took about fifteen hundred years to write the Bible.

- God used more than forty authors to write the Bible. They came from many different backgrounds: kings, fishermen, doctors, politicians, servants, warriors, poets, judges, shepherds, tax collectors, and more.

- The Bible was written in two different parts of the world (Asia and Europe) and in places like a palace and a dungeon, in the wilderness and on a hillside, and even on a road trip while traveling from town to town.

- The Bible was also written in three different languages: Hebrew, Greek, and Aramaic.

- *The Guinness Book of World Records* reports that the Bible holds world records for being the most popular book in history (over 2.5 billion copies on our planet!), and for being the most translated book of all time—available in nearly two thousand different languages.

**What does all this mean? Well . . .
the Bible is *amazing!***

NEW TESTAMENT ADVENTURES

14
Away in a Manger
An adventure about being humble

Matthew 1:18–2:12;
Luke 2:1–20

Howdy, hero!

Earlier this year the Prince of Pride came to town. He said that since he was a prince, everyone should make a big fuss about his arrival. He called my friend Caroline and demanded that she arrange a parade, a marching band, and a row of fancy cars to announce that he had come. He promised Caroline that she could ride right beside him and be famous too! Caroline asked Bibleman what to do, and he reminded her that . . .

Real heroes are humble like Jesus.

Then he told Caroline about the night when Jesus was born.

See these two people? That's Mary on the donkey, and that's Joseph walking beside her. They're headed to Bethlehem right now, but the last nine months have been . . . well . . . a little crazy for them.

It started when the angel Gabriel appeared to Mary and told her, "You have found favor with God! You will give birth to a Son, Jesus. He will be the Son of God."

Mary had questions about that—she wasn't even married yet! But in the end she said, "I'm the Lord's servant. May everything happen just as you've said."

Bethlehem

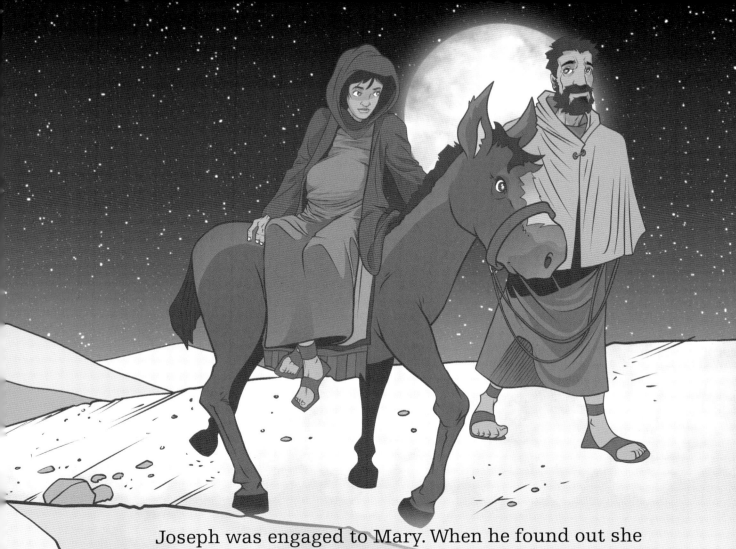

Joseph was engaged to Mary. When he found out she was going to have a baby, he thought he'd have to cancel their wedding. But then an angel visited him in a dream.

"Don't be afraid to take Mary as your wife," the angel said. "She'll give birth to a son, and He will save His people from their sins."

Wow. Joseph obeyed, and soon he and Mary were husband and wife and on their way to Bethlehem for a census.

See where the animals are? That's the humble place where Jesus was born.

When Mary and Joseph arrived in Bethlehem, that was right when it was time for the baby to arrive. There was no room for them anywhere else, so Jesus was born in the place where the animals were kept. Mary wrapped Him in swaddling cloths to keep warm and laid Him in a manger.

In a field nearby, shepherds were watching their flocks by night. A host of angels suddenly appeared! "Today in Bethlehem," they said, "a Savior was born for you!"

The shepherds rushed to Bethlehem and found Baby Jesus in the manger. They were amazed! It was just as the angels had said.

See those three men? We call them "magi" or "wise men."
When Jesus was born, God put a new star in the sky.
These magi from the East saw the star, and they knew
what it meant. God's Son had been born!

They came from far away to meet the humble, new king.
Traveling took a while, but when they found Jesus, the
wise men bowed down and worshiped Him. They gave
Him gifts of gold, frankincense, and myrrh.
Then they left—and most people still didn't
even know that God's great Son had come!

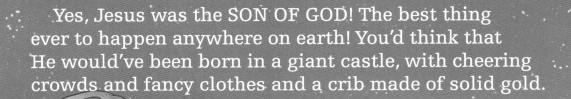

Yes, Jesus was the SON OF GOD! The best thing ever to happen anywhere on earth! You'd think that He would've been born in a giant castle, with cheering crowds and fancy clothes and a crib made of solid gold.

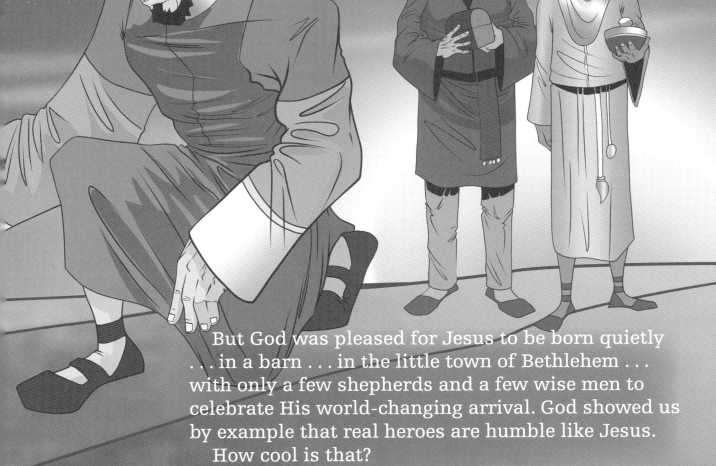

But God was pleased for Jesus to be born quietly . . . in a barn . . . in the little town of Bethlehem . . . with only a few shepherds and a few wise men to celebrate His world-changing arrival. God showed us by example that real heroes are humble like Jesus. How cool is that?

Biblegirl says,

When we're tempted to demand special treatment from others, it's helpful to remember the humble way God chose for Jesus to be born. Instead of being self-centered, we can choose to be real heroes who are humble like Jesus.

That's what Caroline decided to do! Thinking about Jesus' birth helped her resist the Prince of Pride. Instead of giving in to his silly demands for glory, she spent her time volunteering at her church.

Bibleteam Challenge

Design a new Christmas card for your family, no matter what time of year it is! Have your mom or dad write Philippians 2:3 on it, then mail it to your own home. When you receive the card in the mail, have everyone recite the Bible verse aloud together. Then brainstorm three ways you can follow Jesus' humble example this week. Choose one to do tomorrow!

In humility consider others as more important than yourselves.
—*Philippians 2:3*

15
Man of Miracles
An adventure about kindness
Mark 1:40–45; 2:1–12; 8:22–26

Hello, hero! Yesterday was pretty exciting. My friend Corey fell off his skateboard and skinned his knee. It hurt, and Corey was crying a little. Then suddenly the Master of Mean appeared, and he got other kids to make fun of Corey's tears instead of helping him. The Bibleteam jumped into action! Biblegirl told everyone:

Real heroes help others feel better.

Then I opened the Bible, and we read about what Jesus did when others were hurting.

One time, when Jesus was traveling through Galilee, a very sick man met Him on the road. The man had a skin disease called leprosy. It was kind of like having a skinned knee—but all over his body! And it never got better, but always got worse. That poor man was miserable.

"Jesus," the man said, "if You're willing, You can make me better."

Jesus didn't laugh at the man, or chase him away, or make fun of him. Instead, He looked at the man and said, "I am willing. Be clean!"

Bam! The skin disease instantly healed!

That man was so happy he could barely contain himself. He told anyone who would listen, "Jesus healed my disease! Jesus did it—He healed me all over!"

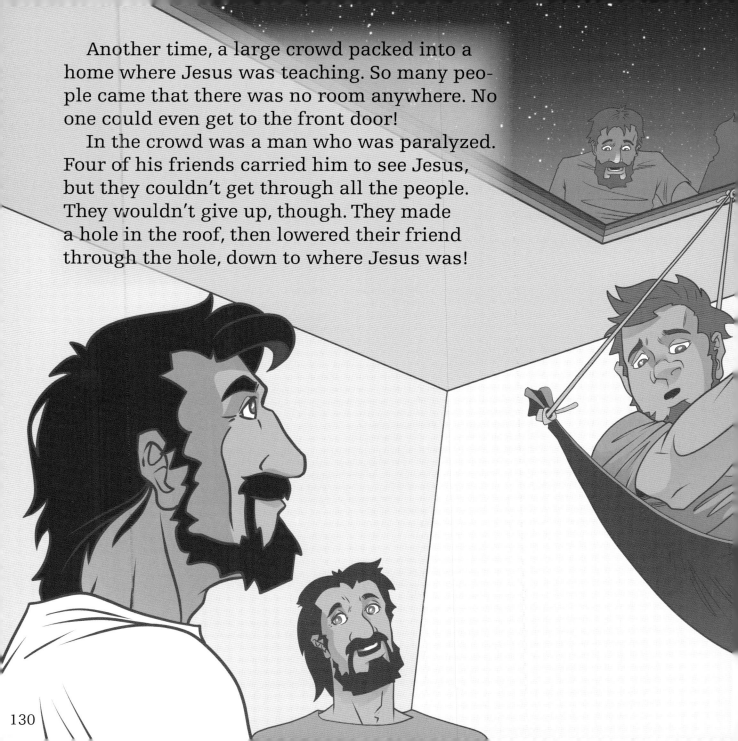

Another time, a large crowd packed into a home where Jesus was teaching. So many people came that there was no room anywhere. No one could even get to the front door!

In the crowd was a man who was paralyzed. Four of his friends carried him to see Jesus, but they couldn't get through all the people. They wouldn't give up, though. They made a hole in the roof, then lowered their friend through the hole, down to where Jesus was!

Jesus saw their faith, and He smiled. "Your sins are forgiven," He said to the paralyzed man. "Get up, take your mat, and go home."

Ka-Pamm! That hurting man was instantly healed. He could walk! He could jump! He could dance and run! He carried his mat out the front door—and the entire crowd was amazed.

And then there was the time when people brought a blind man to Jesus. Life was hard for that poor guy. He couldn't work, people were mean to him, and he had to sit in the street and beg just to get food.

Jesus wanted to help the blind man feel better. He touched the man's eyes once . . .

then twice . . .

then . . .

Wham-a-lam!

The blind man's sight was restored! He saw everything clearly! Once again, Jesus had helped a hurting person to feel better. And you know what? Jesus did this kind of thing All. The. Time!

He is a real, true hero.

Bibleman says,

Jesus is the greatest hero ever. When we take time to look at what He did while on earth, it helps us remember that real heroes help others feel better.

After I told Corey's friends what Jesus' did, they chased the Master of Mean away. They wanted to follow Jesus' example, so two of them helped Corey walk back home so his mom could bandage up that skinned knee. They were real heroes to their friend—and Corey was back to skateboarding before the day was over!

Bibleteam Challenge

Have a parent write the words of Ephesians 4:32 on a sheet of paper or cardboard. Next, cut the paper (or cardboard) into puzzle shapes and mix them up. Spend a few minutes assembling your new puzzle. As you do, answer this question:

"How does Jesus help us feel better today?" Afterward, say Ephesians 4:32 out loud together, then pray, "Jesus, please help us to be real heroes like You are. This week, show us how we can be kind and help others feel better. Amen!"

Be kind and compassionate to one another.
—Ephesians 4:32

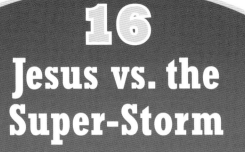

16
Jesus vs. the Super-Storm
An adventure about courage
Mark 4:35–41

Hey there, hero!

A few weeks ago my friend Erik broke his arm when he fell out of a tree. He tried rubbing dirt on it, but that didn't help, so his dad took him to the hospital. Wouldn't you know it? Dr. Fear was hanging out there. That villain told Erik the doctors were going to do all sorts of scary things to him. He was so afraid!

That's when Bibleman showed up. He told Erik about a time when Jesus' disciples were afraid and reminded him that . . .

Real heroes call to Jesus when they need courage.

It was nighttime near the Sea of Galilee, and the end of a long day. Jesus and His disciples packed up their things and headed toward a boat that was waiting for them. They pushed out into the sea. While they were crossing the water, Jesus laid down to take a nap.

But in the distance,
a storm was brewing.

Whooosh! K-k-boooom!
S-s-skkrackkk!

A furious storm hit their boat so fast, the disciples didn't know what to do. They tried to keep the boat afloat. They bailed water and balanced their weight and lowered the sails, but the storm was winning, and they were losing! The wind blew so hard . . . and the lightning cracked so close . . . and the water swamped so high. It looked like the boat was going to sink. Were they all going to drown?

The disciples lost all their courage. They were so, so, so afraid.

"Jesus, wake up!" they shouted at last. "We're going to die! Help us!"

Jesus yawned. He stretched. He stood up and looked around. He wasn't afraid at all, not even a little bit. He said to the sea, "Silence! Be still!"

Immediately the wind
ceased and there was
a great calm on the Sea
of Galilee. "Why are you
afraid?" Jesus asked the
disciples. "Do you still
have no faith?"
    They were stunned.

"Who is this man?" they whispered among themselves. "Even the wind and sea obey Him!" They didn't understand it all, but they had learned one great lesson: when you need courage, the best thing you can do is call to Jesus for help!

Cypher says,

Even Jesus' disciples sometimes felt scared. From their example we learn that real heroes call to Jesus when they need courage. That's something we all need to remember today!

At the hospital, Erik was glad to discover he could call on Jesus for courage about his broken arm. He and Bibleman prayed for Jesus to help, no matter what happened. Jesus answered by giving Erik new strength inside, helping him to be calm while the doctors worked on mending his arm. Dr. Fear was defeated once again!

Bibleteam Challenge

What would happen if you prayed for Jesus to give you courage every day for one week? Try it! This week, when you get up in the morning, get together with your family and pray this prayer: "Jesus, please give us courage to face any fear today. Thank You, Amen!" Before bedtime each night, have everyone tell about how that prayer was answered during the day.

For God has not given us a spirit of fear, but one of power.
—2 Timothy 1:7

142

17
Hungry, Hungry Heroes

An adventure about sharing

John 6:1–13

Hi-ya, hero!

Cypher has spotted the Fibbler sneaking around your neighborhood! Apparently he's telling people that kids can't do anything important for Jesus, that only grown-ups can make a difference for God. Don't believe it, hero! I'm here to tell you that . . .

Kids who share can be real heroes for Jesus!

Here's how I know that's true.

One day Jesus was teaching His disciples about following God. It was so interesting that other people came to listen, and then more people came, and then even more. Pretty soon more than five thousand people were listening to Jesus.

One small boy was part of that really big crowd. He was sitting in one small seat. He was holding one small bag. In that small bag was one small lunch.

Suddenly, Jesus surprised everyone. He turned to His disciple Philip and said, "So, where will we buy bread for all these people to eat?"

Philip almost had a heart attack! "We don't have enough money to buy even one bite of bread for everyone here," he said.

But the little boy was listening, and he thought, *Well, I could share my small lunch, if Jesus wants it.*

He tugged on Andrew's sleeve, and then Andrew said to Jesus, "There's a boy here who has five loaves of bread and two small fish. It's not much, but . . ."

Jesus just grinned. "Have everyone sit down," He said.

Jesus took the bread and fish. He prayed, thanking God for that small lunch and for one small kid who was willing to share what he had with others. And then . . .

He started passing out bread and fish.
Ten people ate their fill. Then a hundred. Then a thousand, then five thousand, and more! Everyone ate bread and fish until they were full—but that little boy's lunch never ran out.

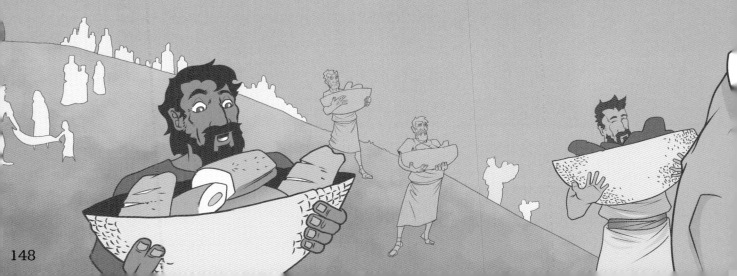

When it was all over, the disciples gathered up the leftovers. There were twelve baskets full of bread and fish! Jesus had worked a fantastic miracle—all because one small boy was willing to share.

How awesome is that?

Melody says,

So you see, that one small boy is proof that kids who share can be real heroes for Jesus!

If the Fibbler comes around your neighborhood and tries to tell you differently, you tell that big ol' liar to get lost! Jesus already used one boy's generosity to work a big miracle—and when you share, He can use you to do important things too.

Bibleteam Challenge

What can you share with others? Go in your room and see if you can find three things to give away to people in need. For instance, maybe you could give away a toy, or a book, or an extra blanket. Show your choices to your parents, and see if you can all brainstorm ways you can share these items this week.

God loves a cheerful giver.
—2 Corinthians 9:7

18
A Lost Boy Found
An adventure about repentance
Luke 15:11–32

Hello, hero!

Mikey knew it was wrong, but the Grand Duchess of Greed told him to do it anyway. So he did. He stole money from his aunt's purse, then ran to the corner store and bought comic books with it.

When the Bibleteam got to the scene, the Grand Duchess was telling Mikey to steal his sister's money next. I knew I had to do something—fast! So I told Mikey about Jesus' parable of the prodigal son and how that story shows us . . .

Real heroes turn away from doing wrong.

The prodigal son lived comfortably on his father's farm. He and his older brother had everything they needed—but that wasn't enough for the prodigal. He was tired of working for his dad. He just wanted to play all day, every day.

"Give me my inheritance now," he said to his father.

It was selfish and wrong to treat his father this way, but he did it anyway. "I've got big plans," he said, "plans to get me far, far away from this boring old farm!"

The father was disappointed, but he granted the son's request. The young man stuffed his bags full of Dad's money and rode away without looking back.

The prodigal boy went to a faraway country. He made it his goal to play-play-play every day-day-day.
But one day . . .

His money ran out.

The party was over—the prodigal was broke! He didn't even have enough cash in his pocket to buy food to eat. To keep from starving, he took a job as a pig-boy, feeding stinky mush to muddy, puddly pigs.

It was *not* fun.

After a while, the prodigal remembered something important.

"I don't have to keep making this same mistake," he told himself. "I can turn away from doing wrong! I'm no longer worthy to be called a son, but maybe my father will make me a hired hand. Even the worst job on my dad's farm is better than feeding stinky slop to pigs."

He dropped his slimy pig pail and headed toward home.

The boy's father saw him coming a long way off. He was so happy!

"Let's celebrate!" Dad said. "I felt like my son was dead, but now he's alive again! He was lost, and now he's found! Hurray!"

So they had a big feast, and the prodigal was home to stay.

Bibleman says,

Hearing Jesus' parable of the prodigal son is a good reminder for us today. Everybody makes bad choices sometimes, but when that happens we can follow the prodigal's example. We can be real heroes who turn away from doing wrong and choose to do what's right instead.

That's what Mikey did. After he learned about what happened to the prodigal son, he stopped listening to the Grand Duchess of Greed. He asked his aunt to forgive him for stealing and then paid her back by doing chores around her house for the next two weeks. Mikey was a real hero!

Bibleteam Challenge

Ask your parents if you can watch a few Internet videos of pigs eating. While you're watching the pigs, talk about the prodigal son.

What do you think it was like when he had to spend all day with pigs? What do you think he would've done differently if he'd known he'd end up as a pig-feeder?

> *Therefore repent and turn back, so that your sins may be wiped out.*
> —*Acts 3:19*

19
Taxman in a Tree
An adventure about judging others
Luke 19:1–10

Hey there, hero!

Yesterday we had a real crisis! The Ambassador of Ignorance showed up at school and started spreading a rumor that anybody who wore green shoes wasn't cool. Next thing we knew, nobody wanted to be friends with any kid wearing green shoes! That really hurt the feelings of those kids, so the Bibleteam ran right over. We held a school assembly and Melody reminded everyone that . . .

Real heroes give anyone a chance to be a friend.

Then she told about Zacchaeus and what happened when he met Jesus.

Zacchaeus was a tax collector who lived in Jericho. In those days, tax collectors were *not* cool. People thought they were mean and greedy, and no one wanted to be their friend.

One day Zacchaeus heard Jesus was passing through town. He was so excited! Zacchaeus really wanted to meet Jesus.

When he got to the road Jesus was walking on, a huge crowd blocked his view. The tax collector was too short to see over all the people!

What'll I do, what'll I do? Zacchaeus wondered.

Then he had an idea.

Zacchaeus ran down the road. He climbed up a tall sycamore tree, settled onto a sturdy branch, and waited.

"Jesus is coming this way," Zacchaeus whispered to himself. "Up here in this tree, I'll see Him clearly when He walks by!"

The crowd came rumbling toward the sycamore tree, closer, closer. And there was Jesus! He was walking alongside His disciples, talking with the people who surrounded Him.

Suddenly He stopped.

He stood right beneath the tree where Zacchaeus was sitting. He looked straight up. And He smiled.

"Zacchaeus," Jesus said. "Hurry and come down. I want to visit your house today."

Zaccheaus was overjoyed to have Jesus visit his house. Some people in Jericho didn't like this idea at all. "Look at Jesus," they grumbled. "Why is He being friends with a tax collector who steals our money? That's *not* cool."

Jesus just ignored them. He gave anyone a chance to be His friend and follow Him—even someone uncool like Zacchaeus. And after meeting Jesus, the tax collector promised never to be mean or greedy again. "Look, Lord!" he said. "I'll give half my possessions to the poor! And if I've cheated anybody out of money, I'll pay back four times as much!"

"Today salvation has come to this house," Jesus said.
    Being friends with Jesus had made a great change in Zacchaeus. On that day, the tax collector followed God with all his heart!

Cypher says,

It's interesting to see that Jesus was willing to be friends with anyone—even someone like Zacchaeus. Learning about that helps us remember that real heroes give anyone a chance to be a friend.

After Melody told the school assembly about Jesus and Zacchaeus, the Ambassador of Ignorance didn't stand a chance. Nobody cared anymore what color shoes their friends wore—they just had fun hanging out together.

Bibleteam Challenge

Can you follow Jesus' example and make a new friend this week? Ask your mom or dad to help you try! Plan a playdate or after-school get-together with two other kids—one person who is already your friend, and one who could be a new friend.

Have fun!

For there is no favoritism with God.
—Romans 2:11

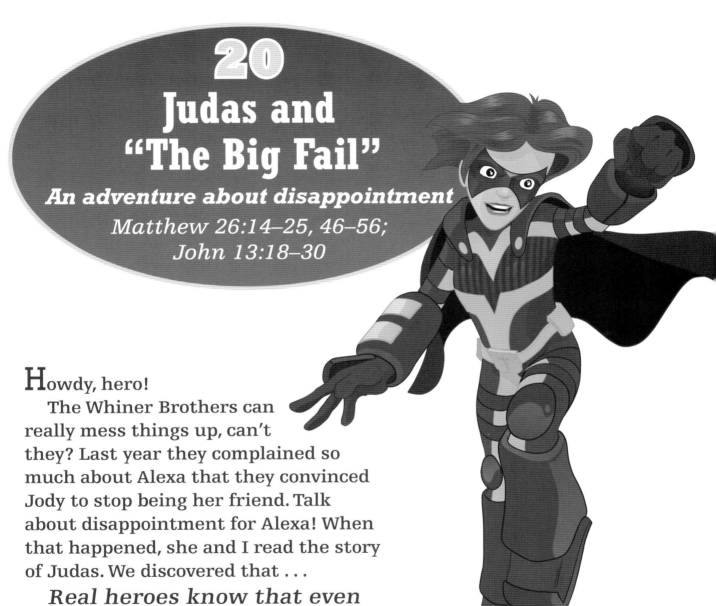

20
Judas and "The Big Fail"

An adventure about disappointment

Matthew 26:14–25, 46–56;
John 13:18–30

Howdy, hero!

The Whiner Brothers can really mess things up, can't they? Last year they complained so much about Alexa that they convinced Jody to stop being her friend. Talk about disappointment for Alexa! When that happened, she and I read the story of Judas. We discovered that . . .

Real heroes know that even when friends disappoint us, God never does.

Here's what happened.

Judas Iscariot was one of Jesus' disciples—one of the top twelve! But Judas figured he deserved more than the other disciples, and sometimes he even stole money from the group.

Then one day he had a really bad idea.

Hmm, he thought, *the chief priests don't like Jesus. They want to arrest Him. Maybe I can make money off that.* So he went to Jesus' enemies and said, "What are you willing to give me if I hand Him over to you?"

The bad guys weighed out thirty pieces of silver for Judas, who started looking for a good time to get Jesus arrested.

A few nights later Jesus was praying quietly in a secret place, in a garden called Gethsemane. Like all of Jesus' disciples, Judas knew that place well. He thought Jesus might have gone there after the supper they had just shared.

It was late when Judas came to Gethsemane. He brought along some goons with swords and torches, sent by the chief priests.

"The guy I kiss on the cheek," he whispered to the goons, "that's Jesus. Arrest Him!"

They arrested Jesus that night, and it was
Judas's fault. Jesus was disappointed in His
friend, but He knew that God was still faithful.
Even when friends disappoint us, God never does.

The next morning Judas was very sorry for what he'd done. He even tried to return the money he got from the chief priests.

But by then, it was just too late.

Biblegirl says,

It's hard to believe, but even Jesus had a friend who was unkind to Him. Such a big disappointment! Jesus could have given up or gotten angry, but He didn't. Jesus knew that even when friends disappoint us, God never does. God is always faithful.

As for Jody, well, the Whiner Brothers won that battle. The girls still aren't friends. But even though she's disappointed, Alexa isn't giving up! She's made new friends, and she keeps praying for Jody.

Bibleteam Challenge

This week, be a faithful friend who encourages instead of a friend who disappoints!

Grab a parent and have a brownie-making spree in your kitchen. While the brownies are baking, have Mom or Dad help you make a list of five friends. Think of one thing you especially like about each friend. When the brownies are ready, put them in gift bags. During the week, give a gift bag to each friend on your list, and tell those friends what you like best about them!

God is faithful.
—1 Corinthians 1:9

Hi-ya, hero!

You know, the Baroness just doesn't get it. That sour old villain told Jennifer that making David feel bad about himself was the way to make Jennifer feel good about herself. That's just not true! Jesus taught us that *loving others* is what really matters, and He proved it when He died on the cross for us. That's why we know that . . .

Real heroes love others like Jesus loved us.

You see, we've all done wrong things—that's called "sin." But God didn't want us to have to suffer the terrible punishment for sin! So God proved His love for us this way: while we were still sinners, Jesus died for us.

The chief priests and religious leaders hated Jesus. After they arrested Him, they took Him to Pilate, the Roman governor where they lived.

"This man must die," they shouted at the governor, "because He claims to be a king! The king of the Jews!" Pilate didn't think Jesus had done anything wrong, but the crowd just shouted louder:

"Take Him away! Take Him away! Crucify Him!"

So Pilate gave the order. And Roman soldiers took Jesus away to die.

Jesus died that day.

It was awful, but it happened because God loved the world so much that He gave His one and only Son, so that everyone who believes in Him will not die but have eternal life instead.

It happened because Jesus loves you and me.

A man named Joseph, from a place called Arimathea, watched Jesus die. He was very sad. He gently took Jesus' body down from the cross and carefully buried Him in a tomb nearby. He rolled a stone in front of the tomb and went away crying.

Joseph didn't know that Jesus' death was NOT the end of this story . . .

Melody says,

Jesus gave everything—even His life—so that we could know God and have eternal life. That's true love! And that's what's really important. Because of Jesus, we understand that real heroes love others like Jesus loved us.

When Jennifer told the Baroness about Jesus and His great love for us, that sour old lady just didn't get it. She couldn't understand why Jennifer would choose to show love to David instead of treating him rudely. But David understood: Jennifer was being a real hero!

Bibleteam Challenge

Jesus showed great love for us when He died on the cross. What are seven different ways you and I can show our love for others this week? Together with your mom or dad, write each of your ideas on a colorful slip of paper and place it in a bowl.

Every day this week, draw an idea out of the bowl and use it to practice showing love to your family members, to your neighbors, to your friends, to people at your church, to the cashier at the supermarket, and to anyone else you think of. Have fun!

God proves his own love for us in that while we were still sinners, Christ died for us.
—Romans 5:8

22
You Can't Keep a God-Man Down!

An adventure about doubt
Matthew 28:1–15; John 20;
1 Corinthians 15:3–8

Hello, hero!

Last Easter the Mayor of Maybe went on a TV talk show and pretended to be an expert on history. "Did Jesus really rise from the dead?" he sneered into the camera. "I doubt it. Did anybody see it? Probably not. I bet His disciples just made up the whole story."

Well, I went down to the TV studio right away. I told everyone the truth:

Real heroes know that Jesus is alive!

And yes, lots of people saw it.

When Jesus was buried, the men rolled a large stone in front of His tomb to close it up. That was on a Friday night.

Sunday morning, one of Jesus' friends, Mary Magdalene, came to the tomb.

Wow—was she surprised!

When Mary got there, she found the stone had been rolled away. The tomb was empty, and a fierce-looking angel was staring at her from on top of the big stone! Gulp!

"Don't be afraid," the angel said. "I know you're looking for Jesus, who was crucified. He's not here! He has risen from the dead. Go quickly, and tell His disciples this good news!"

Mary Magdalene rushed off to tell Jesus' disciples—but what would she say? Did Jesus really come back to life? She didn't know. When she reached the disciples, she said, "They've taken the Lord out of the tomb!"

Those disciples didn't know what to think! They'd seen Jesus die on the cross and be buried . . . so where was His body now? What was going on?

Peter and John had to check it out for themselves. They raced to Jesus' tomb to see if they could figure out what had really happened, and Mary followed behind them.

When Peter and John looked inside the tomb, they didn't know what was going on, but one thing was certain:

Jesus' tomb was empty.

After Peter and John left, Mary stayed behind. What was going on? *Maybe a gardener moved His body?* she thought, and she started to cry.

"Why are you crying?" a voice said. She looked up. At first she thought it was the gardener, and then she realized the truth.

Jesus was alive! He was standing there, right next to her!

But Mary wasn't the only one who saw Jesus. Late that night, the disciples were gathered in a house. They'd locked the doors because they were afraid they might be arrested for being Jesus' friends. All of a sudden . . .

Jesus was there in the house with them! They saw Him with their own eyes!

"Peace be with you," He said to them. Jesus wasn't dead any longer. He was alive forevermore!

Bibleman says,

Over those next few weeks, Jesus actually appeared to a lot of people. Peter saw Him, and all of the disciples did too. One time, over five hundred of Jesus' followers saw Him at the same time! They all witnessed the greatest miracle ever: Jesus had died and then come roaring back to life! And real heroes today know that Jesus is still alive, helping us all.

When the Mayor of Maybe heard about all the witnesses who saw Jesus alive again, he started sweating under the TV studio lights. "Oh," the Mayor said. "Didn't know that. Ahem. Umm. Gotta go."

We didn't hear from the Mayor of Maybe for a long time after that!

Bibleteam Challenge

Go outside and find a few small smooth stones—one for each person in your family. Let each stone represent the large one that once covered Jesus' tomb. As a family, use colored markers to decorate your stones with the words "Jesus is alive!" Then carry your stones in a pocket or purse all week long.

Every time you see your stone, touch it, or just feel it in your pocket, say a prayer to thank God that Jesus is alive today!

For I passed on to you as most important what I also received: that Christ died for our sins according to the Scriptures, that he was buried, that he was raised on the third day.
—1 Corinthians 15:3–4

23
Look, Up in the Sky!
An adventure about trust
Acts 1:1–11; 2:1–40

Hi-ya, hero!

Last year we were volunteering in children's church when all the kids decided to collect five hundred toys to give away to families who didn't have much money. So cool! Then the evil villain Slacker showed up. He said, "That job is too big for a bunch of kids. We'll never collect that many toys. Let's just sit around and play video games instead."

Some of the kids were tempted to listen to that lazy Slacker! So we told everyone:

Real heroes trust in Jesus' Holy Spirit for help.

And we reminded them what happened when Jesus promised to help us.

After Jesus returned to life, He spent forty days encouraging His disciples and teaching them about the kingdom of God.

When it was almost time for Him to return to heaven, Jesus said, "Wait in the city of Jerusalem. In a few days, My Holy Spirit will come to be with you."

And then, while the disciples were standing there watching, Jesus rose into the air. Higher, higher, higher! He disappeared into the sky, returning to heaven where He came from.

Suddenly two angels appeared. "Men of Galilee," they said, "just as Jesus has left for heaven, He will return from heaven again one day!"

A few days later, it was time for a big festival called Pentecost. People from all over the world came to Jerusalem for this holiday. They spoke many different languages, so it was kind of busy and confusing—but it was also an exciting event for everyone.

During the Pentecost celebration, Jesus' disciples gathered together for a meeting and . . .

Something.
Big.
Happened.

They heard a sound like a giant, rushing wind. They saw what seemed like flames rest on each disciple's head.

Jesus had kept His promise—the Holy Spirit had come to help them!

The Holy Spirit filled each man with joy and strength, and they all began speaking in different languages. In the crowd of holiday travelers, people were amazed. Each person heard Jesus' disciples speaking in his or her own language

At last, Peter got up to speak.

"People," he said, "let me explain this to you. Just as He promised, Jesus has given us His Holy Spirit today, a Helper to guide us! Jesus died and was raised from the dead. He is Lord, and His Holy Spirit has come to help us all know Him, love Him, and follow Him."

The people were overjoyed to hear this news. They, too, wanted to follow Jesus!

That day more than three thousand people joined Peter and the disciples. The Holy Spirit had helped them begin a church that would last forever!

Melody and Cypher say,

Reading about the day of Pentecost, when Jesus sent His Holy Spirit, helps us remember that we never have to do anything on our own. Real heroes can always trust in Jesus' Holy Spirit for help!

Slacker still didn't believe we could collect five hundred toys to give away, so he played video games all day. But the rest of us prayed to God for help—then we got to work! We called stores and asked for donations. We prayed some more, then visited our neighbors and friends. We selected the best toys from our own homes and donated them too. We felt the Holy Spirit helping us the whole time. In the end, those kids from children's church collected and gave away . . . 594 toys!

Bibleteam Challenge

With the Holy Spirit's help, do you think your family could help another family in need? This week, pray about that! Ask God to show you new ways to help other families who don't have as much as yours. For instance, you could rake leaves for a neighbor or bake cookies for people at a homeless shelter. At the end of the week, share ideas you got after praying—then pick one for your family to do!

I will ask the Father, and He will give you another Helper, that He may be with you forever.
—*John 14:16* NASB

24
Paul, Prisoner of Rome

An adventure about perseverance
Acts 9:1–31; 27:1–28:32

Howdy, hero!

Well, Luxor Spawndroth came back to town last month. That villain is so tiring. All he wants to do is keep kids from serving Jesus. He tries to make it so hard for them! I remember one time when Brianna wanted to sing a worship song for a local talent show. Luxor was one of the judges of the show, and he threatened to make her leave if she didn't stop singing about Jesus!

I found Brianna crying on the theater steps. I told her not to worry about mean old Luxor because ...

Real heroes never quit serving Jesus.

Then I told her what happened to the apostle Paul.

199

Paul's name used to be Saul. And Saul was *not* a nice guy. He was a lot like Luxor Spawndroth. He hated anyone who followed Jesus! Whenever he got a chance, he arrested Christians and sent them to jail. I'd call that mean.

One time he took a trip to a city called Damascus. He'd heard that Christians were living there, and he wanted to arrest them. But he was in for a surprise.

On the way to Damascus, a bright light suddenly shone down. It was so bright that Saul actually went blind just from looking at it.

Jesus was in the light—and He definitely got Saul's attention. "Who are You, Lord?" Saul said to the light.

"I am Jesus, the one you are trying to hurt," was the answer.

That was all Saul needed to hear. From that day on, all he wanted to do was serve Jesus in everything he did or said.

God restored Saul's eyesight, and after that Saul became a preacher and missionary. He changed his name to Paul, and he traveled the world telling everyone about Jesus. But some people didn't like that. They wanted him to stop. Now.

Paul ignored them. He was determined to serve Jesus, no matter what. So Paul's enemies arrested him. They put him on a boat and sent him to Rome as a prisoner.

Partway to Rome, it started raining. Then it started pouring. Then the wind blew through the boat. Lightning crashed, and everyone on board started worrying that the ship might break apart! The storm lasted for days. Finally Paul stood up. "Don't be afraid," he said. "An angel of God spoke to me last night. This ship will wreck, but God won't let any of us be harmed."

And that's just what happened. The boat was ship-wrecked, but God saved everyone on board.

Paul was finally taken to Rome. He was a prisoner there for two years. So you know what Paul did?

He told his Roman guards about Jesus. He preached about Jesus to anyone who came to see him. He wrote letters about Jesus and sent them to churches all over the land.

Even though he was a prisoner, he still served Jesus boldly! For the rest of his life, no matter how hard it was, the apostle Paul never quit serving Jesus.

Biblegirl says,

We can learn a great lesson from the life and example of Paul. He taught us that even in hard times, real heroes never quit serving Jesus!

After I told Brianna about Paul, she realized that she didn't have to quit serving Jesus just because Luxor Spawndroth was a mean judge at a community talent show. The next day Brianna and her mom took a guitar to the public park next to the theater. They sang worship songs there for anybody who wanted to listen. It was fun—and they attracted quite a crowd! Luxor was defeated again.

Bibleteam Challenge

Make signs to remind you of Paul's life and how he kept serving God even in the toughest times. Gather a few white paper plates, a black marker, and a red marker. In black marker write the word QUIT in the middle of each plate. Then, with the red marker, draw a circle around the word, and put a fat red line through the word QUIT. You've now got your own Don't Quit sign!

Hang your signs on doors all over your home as reminders of what you learned from the apostle Paul.

Be steadfast, immovable, always excelling in the Lord's work.
—1 Corinthians 15:58

25
The Best Is Yet to Come

An adventure about heaven

John 14:1–4;
Revelation 4; 21–22

Hey there, hero!

The Empress of Unhappiness is never satisfied unless everyone else is sad. This morning she set up a karaoke machine downtown—but instead of singing, she just kept saying, "Aren't you tired of so many bad things in the world? Tornadoes and sickness and broken toys! There's nothing to do but be sad, sad, sad!"

By the time I got there, people were crying all over the sidewalk. So I stepped up to the microphone with good news! We don't have to be sad like people with no hope because . . .

Real heroes know Jesus is preparing heaven for us!

The apostle John told us all about it.

207

John was one of Jesus' trusted disciples. When John was an old man, he was sent to live on a prison-island called Patmos. It was a hard place to live—but while he was there, something really cool happened.

An angel appeared to John! "Come up here," the angel said. "I'll show you what is going to happen one day."

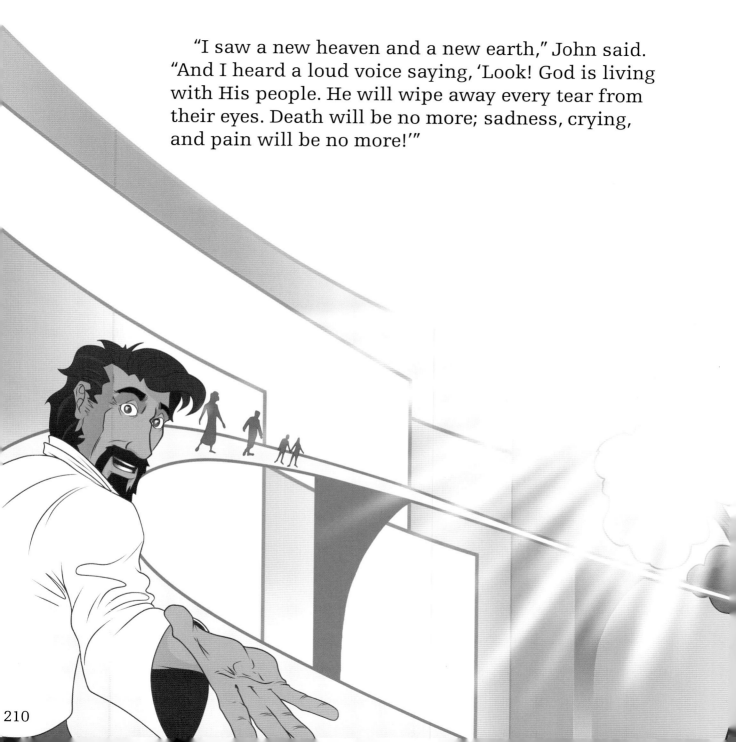

"I saw a new heaven and a new earth," John said. "And I heard a loud voice saying, 'Look! God is living with His people. He will wipe away every tear from their eyes. Death will be no more; sadness, crying, and pain will be no more!'"

"Write this down," God said to John, "because this promise is faithful and true: Look! I am making everything new."

211

Then an angel carried John to a high mountain. From there he saw a brand-new city coming down from the sky.

God had made a New Jerusalem, a place for His people to enjoy with Him forever.

Wow, it was beautiful.

A crystal-clear river flowed through the middle of the city. The River of Life! And on both sides of the river was the Tree of Life. It was like the garden of Eden had been created all over again. God was making everything new.

And John saw Jesus, waiting to bring us into His wonderful heaven. "I am coming soon," Jesus promised.

"Amen!" John said. "Come, Lord Jesus!"

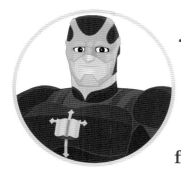

Bibleman says,

When we feel worried about all the sad and bad things that are happening in our world, the apostle John can encourage us. He reminds us that real heroes know Jesus is preparing a wonderful heaven for us—and that Jesus is coming soon to share His great heaven with us.

So when I was downtown and told the Empress of Unhappiness what I knew about heaven, she frowned at me. "Wait a minute," she said. "Heaven isn't a sad thing. It actually sounds great." She sighed as she packed up her karaoke machine. "Guess I'll have to go find something else to make me unhappy."

"Yep," I said. And everyone cheered as she left!

Bibleteam Challenge

Go on a "Heavenly Photo Scavenger Hunt." Over the next week, look for things that remind you of heaven and take pictures of them. You might take a photo of a beautiful sunset, a crystal-clear river, an impressive tree, or anything else that makes you think of heaven. (Be sure to include yourself in some of your pictures!)

Print your favorite images, and keep them all in a photo album so you can look at them whenever you want to give yourself an encouraging reminder of heaven.

Look, I am coming soon!
—Revelation 22:7

Remember:

Put on the full armor of God, so that you can stand against the schemes of the devil.—*Ephesians 6:11*

Read:

Did you know that God gives you armor? You can read about it in Ephesians 6:10–17. The Sword of the Spirit is one of the pieces of armor. It's a way of describing the Word of God, the Bible! So that means the Bible is armor you can use to fight against temptation and sin. The more you read its words and learn from it, the more you know God and the stronger you become.

God knows you will have many battles to fight in life as you learn to follow Him. Always rely on His Word—His armor—to give you strength and protect you.

Think:

1. Which Bible story adventure is your favorite? What can you learn from it?

2. Think of three words that describe a hero. Do those words describe Jesus? Do they describe you?

3. The Bibleteam uses the Bible to fight for the truth and tell others about Jesus. How can you use God's Word to teach others too?

4. Make a list of some challenges you might face in the next few months: jealousy, fear, anger, sadness. Can you think of people in the Bible who felt the same way? What can you learn from them?

5. How is Jesus the biggest hero of all?

DON'T MISS ANY OF THE BIBLETEAM'S OTHER ADVENTURES!

AVAILABLE NOW WHEREVER BOOKS ARE SOLD!

B&H KIDS